COMING TO JESUS

Giving a Good
INVITATION

"Coming to Jesus: Giving a Good Invitation" is the expanded and revised version of Dr. Roy J. Fish's "Giving a Good Invitation," published in 1974.

ROY J. FISH

▶ ▶ ▶

"Because the invitation to trust Christ is God's idea, rather than man's, it is worthy of both consideration and implementation today. Roy Fish's book, *Coming to Jesus: Giving a Good Invitation*, comes from the heart of a man who remains the most passionate winner of souls to Jesus I have ever met. As his student, friend and co-laborer in God's harvest field, I can assure you that every principle in this book comes from the heart of God. This study, the last in his storied lifetime, was first hammered out on the anvil of Roy Fish's own life. You will be blessed, and your ministry will be bettered by having immersed yourself in the pages of this book."

-Tom Elliff
President, International Mission Board, Southern Baptist Convention

"Dr. Roy Fish was the greatest evangelism professor Southern Baptists have ever had. He was also one of our preeminent evangelists, a fruitful practitioner of all that he taught. Including an invitation turns each worship service into an evangelistic event. From this marvelous resource you will learn the origins and theology of the invitation, and you will learn how to use it properly and effectively in your church. You will not find a more useful resource to help you introduce people to Christ week by week in your worship services. May God bless every pastor and evangelist who reads this essential book!"

-Chuck Kelley
President, New Orleans Baptist Theological Seminary

"Fishers of men fish, and that entails drawing the net. Jesus instructed His disciples to do that and it applies until His appearing. The greatest act of worship is to love Him and to publish the gospel as a witness to all nations so then the end will come. Complete witness requires an invitation to come to Jesus. This book biblically explains the idea of an invitation succinctly, clearly, and vividly. Every student, layperson, pastor, teacher, evangelist, or missionary needs to digest and apply thoroughly the contents of this monograph."

-Keith E. Eitel
Dean of Roy J. Fish School of Evangelism and Missions,
Southwestern Baptist Theological Seminary

"I had the great opportunity to discuss the issues addressed in *Coming to Jesus: Giving a Good Invitation* with Dr. Fish on several occasions during the last few years of his life. He very often expressed great concern at the lack of urgency among Christians for reaching the lost! He especially felt this way when it came to the unwillingness of God's man to effectively invite the unsaved to genuine repentance and biblical faith. For Dr. Fish, it was nothing short of spiritual malpractice for one to powerfully exegete the Word of God and at the same time, to not put as much spiritual preparation into the invitation! In *Coming to Jesus*, Dr. Fish addresses the lost art of giving a good invitation by providing practical suggestions that will enhance communication and bring more expectancy to the close of the sermon."

-David A. Wheeler
Professor of Evangelism,
Liberty University and Liberty Baptist Theological Seminary.

"As a young evangelist I read *Giving a Good Invitation* again and again. The insights I learned as a young man I still employ today. I welcome this revised edition of the work of my mentor and hero Roy Fish. It will inform, inspire, and ignite you to share the good news!"

-Alvin L. Reid
Professor of Evangelism and Student Ministry/Bailey Smith Chair of Evangelism,
Southeastern Baptist Theological Seminary.

"*Coming to Jesus* by the late Dr. Roy Fish is a modern classic on giving public invitations to decide for Jesus Christ. This book, with its heart and theology, should be read by all who are privileged to preach the eternal gospel of salvation in Jesus Christ. Any sermon on the Savior should end with His divine invitation to 'Come!' It is my prayer that this book will be mightily used of God to encourage His servants in the harvest fields!"

-Thomas P. Johnston
Professor of Evangelism, Midwestern Baptist Theological Seminary

"Dr. Roy Fish was my professor, mentor, and friend. He lived with a red-hot passion to see people put their faith and trust in Jesus Christ as Savior and Lord. In this book he discusses a variety of ways to invite persons to respond to the gospel message, but the central theme is his passion to see persons saved. You may not agree with all these approaches, but adopt his passion! I am glad you are putting this book out in your dad's honor. He touched so many lives, and this book will continue his impact for years to come."

-Timothy K. Beougher
Associate Dean, Billy Graham School of Missions, Evangelism and Ministry;
Billy Graham Professor of Evangelism and Church Growth,
Southern Baptist Theological Seminary

"From the latter half of the twentieth century to the present, Southern Baptists have associated Dr. Roy Fish with the art of inviting others to come to Jesus. Before he went to be with Jesus, one of his last wishes was that *Coming to Jesus: Giving a Good Invitation* be published. Many educators in the field of evangelism, pastors, and former students shared this same wish. Thanks to the effort and determination of Dr. Fish's family, all of us have seen our wish come true.

"In *Coming to Jesus*, Dr. Fish leaves following generations the textbook on extending an evangelistic invitation. Tracing the biblical, historical, and philosophical bases for the evangelistic invitation, *Coming to Jesus* offers readers instruction about and reasons for the importance of the public invitation to receive Christ."

-Matt Queen
The Lee R. Scarborough Chair of Evangelism (Chair of Fire),
Assistant Professor of Evangelism and Associate Dean for Doctoral Programs,
Roy Fish School of Evangelism and Missions,
Southwestern Baptist Theological Seminary

"For biblical and practical help on how to give a public invitation, this revised work of a classic by the legendary Roy Fish remains unsurpassed. I will never forget the classes I had under Dr. Fish at Southwestern Seminary in the late 1970s. His heart throbbed with the love of God for the lost, and his passion to motivate his students was unmatched. This work should be on every pastor's shelf."

-David L. Allen
Dean of the School of Theology and Professor of Preaching,
Southwestern Baptist Theological Seminary

"I never dreamed that I would see the day in my own denomination that the public gospel invitation would fall into disfavor, be disdained, and even 'demonized' by some. While the debate rages about the utilization of the invitation in evangelistic preaching as well as personal witnessing among evangelicals, the lost are plunging headlong into hell in droves. Recently a call was extended to Southern Baptists for a Great Commission Resurgence. What is desperately needed now among Southern Baptists and all evangelical denominations is a gospel Invitation Resurgence! Dr. Roy Fish is leading the way for such a Gospel Invitation Resurgence in the revised and updated version of his classic work on the gospel invitation. In his re-titled book *Coming to Jesus: Giving a Good Invitation*, Dr. Fish reminds us of the biblical and historical precedents for extending gospel invitations as well as the spiritual, practical, and even sound psychological reasons for inviting the lost to respond publicly to the Gospel. If you have begun to waver as to the necessity of the public invitation, feel as though your extension of public invitations has become stale and routine, or you simply want to improve the way in which you make the public appeal for salvation decisions, you need to read this book and apply the principles contained therein. What Dr. Fish shares in *Coming to Jesus* will renew your passion for the public gospel invitation and revitalize your practice of extending the invitation in order that more might come to Christ under your proclamation ministry. My prayer is that the Lord will use Dr. Fish's revised work on the gospel invitation, completed by his precious wife and children after his death, to contribute to a Gospel Invitation Resurgence that will result in millions more lost souls ushered into the Kingdom before Jesus comes again! I thank Dr. Roy Fish, my mentor, hero, and friend for his timely word on this critical issue in the church today."

-*Preston L. Nix*
The Roland Q. Leavell Chair of Evangelism,
Professor of Evangelism and Evangelistic Preaching,
New Orleans Baptist Theological Seminary

Book design by Sharayah Colter, Colter & Co. Design
Fort Worth, Texas
www.colterco.com

Cover image © Shutterstock

Library of Congress Control Number: 2015914221
CreateSpace Independent Publishing Platform, North Charleston, SC

ISBN-13: 978-1516902118
ISBN-10: 1516902114

Table of Contents

Foreword

One day a young farmer was busily removing fence posts. This young farmer had taken over the family farm soon after his father's death. He surmised that the land was fertile and would be perfect for raising crops. While he was removing the fence posts, a neighbor came by. He asked the young man what he was doing. The young farmer replied, "I'm preparing this field to plant cotton. My dad used it for raising cattle, but I plan to make a lot more money raising crops like cotton, corn, and soy beans." The neighboring farmer replied, "Son, before you remove those fence posts, have you tried to plow that field?"

The young farmer answered, "Well, no. Why?"

The neighbor smiled and said, "Because that land is filled with huge boulders just below the surface. There aren't two inches of topsoil at any spot on that field. That's why your old dad used it to graze cows. Son, it's always the better part of wisdom to ask someone why a fence was built before you start tearing it down."

You and I live in a day when age-old "fences" are being torn down almost daily. Many are now arguing that the age-old "fence" of Biblical marriage (one man married to one woman for life) needs to be torn down. In America, states are beginning to legalize drugs like marijuana, which in the past have been wisely viewed as dangerous to society and harmful to one's health. Yet, to many, such "fences" seem obsolete and out of place.

Sadly, the same mentality seems to be moving into Christian churches. Today, church leaders and members are sometimes eager to tear down ancient ecclesiastical and theological fences without ever asking why they were originally erected. In some Christian circles, the mentality seems to be, "If it's new, it's good, and if it's old, it's bad."

To be sure, methods of "doing church" change as years slip by. C.H.

FOREWORD

Spurgeon probably would not preach today the exact same way that he did in London in the late 1800s. Spurgeon was "a man for all time" because he was "a man for his time." There is nothing wrong with modern preachers utilizing up-to-date technology in order to be relevant and enhance their sermon delivery. We must always seek to take a never-changing gospel to an ever-changing world. Nevertheless, there are some "fences" in Christian ministry that should not be removed.

For instance, preachers must never neglect preaching about the exclusivity of salvation in Jesus Christ. Similarly, preachers must never stop sharing the gospel with lost people (non-Christians) when they preach in order to win them to Jesus Christ as Savior and Lord. These "fences" are too foundational to Christianity to ever be removed.

In a similar vein, I would suggest that preachers should always preach sermons that end with some form of invitation to allow their listeners to respond then and there to the claims they have just heard regarding the gospel of Jesus Christ. That is a biblical fence that should always be left standing. Such invitations in sermons are on the decline. More and more preachers seem to be shying away from "altar calls." They recoil at the idea of calling people to respond publicly to the truth they proclaim. Many preachers consider a "come forward, evangelistic invitation" to be little more than an antiquated scare tactic. They say that such invitations are unnecessary and even unbiblical.

Wait just a minute! Did any of the biblical preachers ever extend any sort of public invitation? Absolutely! If, then, public invitations such as these are found in Scripture, why would anyone seek to tear down such important fences? There have always been various types of public invitations. The issue at stake is not to try to establish one exclusive way of publicly inviting people to Christ. The real issue (the fence that must not be moved) is that whenever the gospel is preached, the listeners should be invited then and there to repent of their sin, believe in Jesus, and call upon the name of the Lord to be saved. Preaching without inviting people to Christ is simply unbiblical.

One of the best works regarding the public invitation ever to be written came from the brilliant mind and burning heart of Dr. Roy Fish. For over 40 years, Dr. Fish taught Evangelism at Southwestern Baptist Theological Seminary in Fort Worth, Texas. He served as a preacher, evangelist, pastor, and professor. In the mid-1970s, he published a book titled *Giving a Good Invitation*. His work is a masterpiece, providing biblical support for public invitations as well as practical guidance and wisdom in how to effectively extend them. I am pleased to be writing the foreword to this updated version of his original book.

Dr. Fish trained more students in Evangelism than any other professor in history. I had the privilege of serving as his grader at Southwestern Seminary from 1981-88. For over thirty years he was my professor, mentor, ministerial confidant, example, prayer partner, and beloved friend. This year I have entered into my thirtieth consecutive year of serving as a senior pastor in Baptist churches. I began preaching five years before that, which means that for some thirty-five years I have publicly called men, women, boys, and girls to follow Jesus. One constant source of joy and encouragement in my ministry has been to preach the Word of God, extend an open invitation, and watch the Holy Spirit work in the hearts of the listeners.

As best I can calculate, I have extended over 5,000 public invitations for people to receive Christ as Savior and Lord. By God's grace, I have watched as thousands have been saved as a result. Virtually everything I know about extending public invitations comes from the teachings of my esteemed friend, Dr. Roy Fish.

Fish's book on giving public invitations is a classic – a time-tested fence. Every preacher would do well to digest the truths regarding this all-important subject set forth so simply and Scripturally in this small, but potent work. It was written by one of the most humble, holy, happy, Christ-like men ever to live. The epitaph about Abel is also true about Roy Fish: "Though he is dead, he still speaks" (Heb. 11:4).

Any communicator of the gospel would be wise to allow this great man of God to speak into his life. Allow Dr. Fish to show you why every gospel preacher should conclude every sermon by "Giving a Good Invitation."

3 John 2,
Steve Gaines, Ph.D.
Senior Pastor, Bellevue Baptist Church
Memphis, Tennessee

Preface

One of the most beautiful words in the entire Bible is the word "come." It is found in the early chapters of Genesis when God said to Noah, "Come into the ark, you and all your household" (Gen. 7:1) and throughout the Bible to the last chapter when the universal invitation was given: "And the Spirit and the bride say, 'Come!' And let him who hears say, 'Come!' And let him who thirsts come. Whoever desires, let him take the water of life freely" (Rev. 22:17).

The word "come" is a word of invitation, so one might accurately say the Bible begins with an invitation and concludes in the same way. The Bible is the story of God inviting sinful people to come and receive the benefits of the redemptive work of the Lord Jesus Christ. R. T. Kendall, in his excellent work *Stand Up and Be Counted*, refers to the public invitation as "calling men out of hiding." If this is the case,

God first began calling people out of hiding in the Garden of Eden. Immediately after Adam and Eve ate the forbidden fruit, "the eyes of them both were opened, and they knew that they were naked." They thus sewed fig leaves together and made coverings for themselves. Then they heard the voice of the Lord God in the cool of the day, and Adam and his wife hid themselves from the presence of the Lord God amongst the trees of the garden" (Gen. 3:7-8). Sin always leads one to retreat into hiding ... The task of every minister is to address men and women in this willful darkness and hiding. That is what God did in Eden. "And the Lord God called unto Adam, and said unto him, where art thou?" (Gen. 3:9).[1]

The word "invitation" in nontheological language is one commonly used and easily understood. We talk in terms of inviting someone over for a visit or an invitation to a special occasion. Most people do not have difficulty understanding the word when used like this.

In theological and particularly evangelistic terms, the invitation is an appeal to someone to accept the benefits of the Christian gospel. These benefits include forgiveness of sin, a new quality of life, peace, purpose, life everlasting, and much more. Since these benefits come through a person, an evangelistic invitation is an appeal to accept this person, Jesus Christ, into one's life as Savior and Lord.

As a rule, among most evangelicals, the word "invitation" includes prescribing some specific action in the way of external expression of a positive response. However, the word "invitation" encompasses more than this. It includes any appeal to repent and to respond affirmatively to Jesus. It could be signing a card, raising a hand, or standing. It could be as unobtrusive as inviting people to pray where they are standing or sitting and simply appealing to them to put their trust in Jesus Christ with no opportunity given for public expression.

The invitation as discussed in this book will generally include specifying some external form of positive response to the gospel. Assuming the conditions for receiving salvation have been clearly expressed, the invitation will be defined as an appeal to meet these conditions and to openly demonstrate one's willingness to do so by taking some specific action described by the preacher. Traditionally, this action has been coming forward to the front of an auditorium or church building to indicate that one is receiving Christ or making some other commitment to Him.

-Roy J. Fish
Southwestern Baptist Theological Seminary

Acknowledgements

Roy Fish went to be with the Lord on September 10, 2012. One of his last desires was for this book to be published. He would want to thank his beloved wife, Jean, who worked on this new edition of his book and helped his dream come to fruition. She was aided in this effort by Steve Fish, Holli Fish Lancaster, and Jennifer Fish Pastoor. Many thanks also go to Brittany Jones, Dr. Matt Queen, and Brandon Kiesling for help with the endnotes.

Introduction

Although public invitations have been a vital part of the services in many evangelical churches, printed material dealing with the subject is notably sparse. In an exhaustive doctoral dissertation on the subject written in 1979, Oscar Thompson noted that he had found only two books that had ever been written specifically on the subject.[2]

Ironically, most pastors are quick to admit that giving an invitation is perhaps the weakest part of their platform ministry. Most of them readily confess that they need help in this crucial area. This need was the primary reason for my writing, in 1974, the small monograph, *Giving a Good Invitation*.[3] The book was published by Broadman Press and stayed in print over twenty years. At one time it was in Broadman's top ten books as far as sales were concerned.

Since that writing, to my knowledge, only two books have been written in this country on the subject: R. Alan Streett's fine work, *The Effective Invitation*[4] and the splendid contribution of O. S. Hawkins, *Drawing the Net*.[5] An American pastor who now ministers in England, R. T. Kendall, has written a superb book on the subject, *Stand Up and Be Counted*,[6] but being published in England, it has not had wide circulation in this country. The same is true of a book published by an Australian scholar, *The Altar Call*,[7] by David Bennett. The dearth of literature concerning such a vital part of preaching still exists.

Since my first book on this subject, some significant and sometimes rather drastic changes have occurred in the nature of public invitations. A number of pastors have stopped giving public invitations altogether; others have changed their methods to the degree that they have ceased to invite people to "come forward" in traditional public confession.

Not only have changes occurred, but also a new generation of pastors has come on the scene who have little or no printed material to guide them in this part of ministry. These factors have led to my desire to rewrite and expand the book I wrote some thirty-five years ago.

As I stated in my original book, no one walks with the presumptuous step of a know-it-all when dealing with this vital subject. Anyone who approaches it likely does so with a rather keen sense of inadequacy. Anyone who writes on the subject is indebted, not only to the afore-mentioned books, but to the several authors who have included chapters on the invitation in books written on the general subject of evangelism.

When speaking on this subject at Baptist evangelism conferences, or in meetings of an interdenominational nature, I have found pastors of all denominations extremely interested and have also found the subject to be of extreme interest in classes I teach at Southwestern Seminary.

I am convinced that every minister of the gospel can learn how to give a good invitation. Admittedly, every preacher might not have some innate ability that will make him a great preacher, but almost without exception each one can give a strong invitation. It is something that can be learned. It is with the hope that this book will add to the learning process that this manuscript is set forth.

-Roy J. Fish
Southwestern Baptist Theological Seminary

The Biblical Basis of the Invitation

Though seldom discussed with any degree of thoroughness, the key question relative to the invitation is, "Is there a biblical basis for it?" Does precedent exist in the Bible for calling people to a public, "on the spot" decision regarding some aspect of their relationship to God? Faris Whitesell, former Professor at Northern Baptist Theological Seminary–in what for years was the most definitive work on this subject–asserts that the spirit and principle of the invitation are biblical. This is his primary argument for its justification:

> True enough, we do not find an exact example of the modern evangelistic invitation in the Scriptures, but this fact does not condemn it as unscriptural. Many Christian practices and institutions now in use are not mentioned in the Scriptures; yet we do not consider them unscriptural. We find no references in the Bible to Sunday schools, women's missionary organizations, church buildings, ushers, hymnbooks, offering envelopes, church bulletins, church pews and the like, but who would cast them all aside for this reason? Anything that helps us carry out the principles and teachings of the Scriptures in a more effective and practical way is scriptural. The evangelistic invitation does exactly that: it is a practical aid in bringing men to Christ openly and publicly, and that work, according to the New Testament, is the main business of Christians.[8]

In my opinion, Whitesell does not go far enough. There is far more explicit evidence for extending invitations in the Bible than something that "helps us carry out the principles and teachings of the Scriptures in a more effective and practical way," as Whitesell says. A perusal of the Old and New Testaments will demonstrate the pervasiveness of the invitation. Because there is an essential difference in the desired object and nature of the appeal in the invitations in the Old Testament and the New, the two shall be treated separately.

Old Testament

The Bible itself is a virtual invitation for people to come to the Lord, so it is not surprising to find explicit invitations offered in the Old Testament. The Old Testament includes at least six specific invitations for people to make public decisions concerning their relationship with God. These will be examined chronologically with a brief description of each one, along with an analysis of common factors.

Before looking at what I call "explicit invitations" in the Old Testament, it should be observed that R. T. Kendall suggests that the night of the Passover represents a response to an invitation which had come from God through Moses. "It was a visible demonstration of their obedience – it was a public pledge. It was their pledge to God and God's pledge to them and it was their witness before the world."[9] This, however, is not quite as explicit as other invitations found in the Old Testament.

The first of these explicitly stated invitations happened after the people of God lapsed into idolatry by worshipping a golden calf while Moses was on the mountain receiving the tablets of the law. When Moses came down from the mountain and saw the sinful orgy in which the people were engaged, the Bible says, "Then Moses stood in the entrance to the camp, and said, "Whoever is on the Lord's side – come to me!" (Ex.32:26). This appeal is a very explicit invitation to publicly demonstrate that one would continue to follow the Lord. Kendall suggests that this incident might be used as justification for inviting people to publicly rededicate their lives to God.[10]

The second of these invitations occurred after the people of Israel had conquered the land of Canaan. A time of spiritual crisis arose which demanded a renewal of the covenant. At this juncture, Joshua, the successor of Moses, challenged the people with the well-known words, "choose for yourselves this day whom you will serve ... " (Josh. 24:15). And when the people indicated verbally that they would choose the Lord, Joshua insisted on a public demonstration of their commitment. Whitesell says: "Joshua called for public decision on the part of the people ... and had it recorded and memorialized so they could never forget."[11]

To a somewhat indecisive congregation, the prophet Elijah extended an obvious invitation at a time when the nation of Israel had become deeply involved in the worship of Baal. In his courageous open challenge to both Baal and the people of Israel, the prophet issued the following invitation: "How long will you falter between two opinions? If the Lord is God, follow Him; but if Baal, then follow him" (1 Kings 18:21). At that point no one responded to his invitation, but when God manifested Himself in falling fire that consumed the sacrifice, the people responded to his invitation by falling on their faces and saying, "The Lord, He is God! The Lord, He is God!" (1 Kings 18:39). The public further reacted to his challenge by seizing the prophets of Baal and taking them to the brook Kishan where Elijah slew them.

More than once, public invitations were extended in the Old Testament when there was a serious need to renew Israel's initial covenant with God. Such was the case when the Book of the Law, lost for several decades, was found during the repair of the Temple building. King Josiah made a new commitment to follow God's law: "And he made all who were present in Jerusalem and Benjamin take a stand" (2 Chron. 34:32). Josiah did not seem to be afraid of "putting too much pressure" on his people to get them to decide.

The last two appeals for public response in the Old Testament occurred during the Post-Captivity Revival under Ezra and Nehemiah. The first involved the renunciation of flagrant acts of disobedience of the Law of God. Ezra required the people to swear an oath that they would do according to this word: "So they swore an oath" (Ezra 10:5). In Nehemiah 9:38 Nehemiah required people to place their seal on a document of new commitment to God, something that was tantamount to affixing one's signature on a pledge.

These Old Testament invitations show the heart of God, which continually implores people to choose Him and His ways. From these examples, we can generalize certain elements that characterize Old

3

Testament invitations. Though these characteristics are not noted in every one of the appeals studied, they highlight important aspects of the Old Testament invitations.

First of all, *every invitation involved a choice* on the part of individuals who comprised the groups to whom invitations were extended. Though the word "choose" is found only in the invitation of Joshua to the people of Israel, personal choice is an implied part of every one of them. God did not allow for neutrality. The people were "for God" or "against God."

Second, *a variety of methods were employed* in the way people were called on to respond to appeals. At times, the primary response was simply a verbal commitment, as in the case of Joshua and Elijah. Moses invited people to come to the place where he was standing if they were really on the Lord's side. Nehemiah insisted that people sign a pledge. Preachers offering invitations today should seriously consider this variety and prayerfully decide which methods they will employ.

Third, *the leaders expected an immediate response*. When Joshua exhorted the people to choose, he did not tell them to "go home and think it over." There is no reason to believe in any of the above instances that the leaders gave the people opportunity to deliberate for any length of time.

Fourth, *response to every one of these invitations was publicly demonstrated*. There is no record of a "secret, done in the heart only" type of dedication. Leaders asked people to come, to stand, to verbally commit, to swear an oath–all in the presence of other people.

Fifth, *the imperative was employed periodically in leading people to follow God*. When Josiah had made a new covenant to follow and obey the Lord, he commanded his people to "take their stand for it." Similarly, in the New Testament Paul said, "God . . . commands all men everywhere to repent" (Acts 17:30). In the Old and New Testaments, God uses human instruments to proclaim His message and command people to come to Him.

New Testament

Because of the difference in the way God deals with people in the New Testament as compared to the Old, there is a corresponding difference in the nature of the invitations in the two. The basic difference is that the invitation in the New Testament always relates in one way or another to Jesus. Invitations were inevitably a call to allegiance to Him.

Jesus Himself extended invitations that called for a public response of commitment to Him. Surprisingly enough, the first invitation He extended was not to Peter and Andrew, but to Philip of Bethsaida. The Scriptures are bright and succinct at this point: "[Jesus] found Philip and said to him, 'Follow me'" (John 1:43). He used the same words in inviting Peter and Andrew, then James and John to be his followers (Matt. 4:18-22). He did the same with Matthew (Matt. 9:9). Zacchaeus responded to a public invitation and came down from a tree to follow Jesus (Luke 19:1-10). As a rule, those who were so invited responded positively to the call. As far as the New Testament record reveals, only one person, the rich young ruler, declined the invitation to follow when the appeal was extended in this manner (Matt. 19:16-22).

In his dissertation, Thompson suggests of Matthew 11:28-29:

It is possible that Jesus had some kind of public commitment in mind when He said, "Come unto me, all who are weary and heavy-laden, and I will give you rest. Take my yoke upon you, and learn from me, for I am gentle and humble of heart: and ye shall find rest for your souls. For my yoke is easy, and my load is light."[12]

In the parable of the ignored dinner invitation, Jesus has the master of the house commanding servants to "Go out into the highways and along the hedge and compel them to 'come in'" (Luke 14:23 NASB). The word *angkoson,* here translated as "compel," is a strong word; yet the opportunity or privilege of declining still belonged to the person invited to the dinner. The real test to justify the biblical basis of the public invitation is the ministry of the apostles as it is seen in the book of Acts. Unquestionably Peter extended some type of public invitation after preaching his sermon at Pentecost. It is provable both contextually and lexically. Contextually, the narrative in Acts 2 states that "those who had received his word were baptized; and that day there were added about three thousand souls" (Acts 2:41 NASB). The question, which confronts the reader of the book of Acts at this point, is: How did Peter know whom to baptize out of the huge crowd which heard him? The only possible answer is that some type of public response to his appeal was called for, which seems to be adequate contextual proof for justifying invitations biblically.

Further proof comes from the lexical aspect of the passage. The text says regarding Peter, "with many other words did he testify and exhort" (Acts 2:40). The word "exhort" translated is the Greek word *parakaleo* from which comes the word *paraklete*. This is in keeping with *A Greek English Lexicon of the New Testament* which, in its entry for *parakaleo*, says, "To ask to come and be present where the speaker is."[13] It doesn't take much sanctified imagination to see Simon Peter calling to himself those who are willing to obey his injunction to repent.

C. E. Autrey observes:

> Peter delivered the body of his sermon and had reached the climax which is described in the following words, "and with many other words did he testify and exhort." His invitation may have contained as many words and illustrations as the body of the sermon. The length of the time of pleading is not the point, but the fact that he actually exhorted the people to act upon what they had heard is very significant. Peter was as much under the direction of the Holy Spirit while he exhorted as when he preached. The evangelist is not pushing the Holy Spirit aside when he pleads in the invitation any more than when he prepares and delivers the body of the sermon.[14]

Further evidence is seen in the ministry of the Apostle Paul. In Ephesus, "He entered the synagogue and continued speaking out boldly for three months, reasoning and persuading them about the kingdom of God" (Acts 19:8 NASB). Whitesell sees persuasion here as being invitation and contends that baptism in the early church was commensurate to the public profession of faith today. Concerning Paul's ministry in Ephesus, Whitesell concludes: "If he did not use our methods of invitation, he must have used something akin to them."[15]

This brief survey through the Old and New Testaments confirms the biblical basis of the public invitation. Defending the practices ceases to be necessary. Those who believe the Bible should take the offensive and challenge those who do not give opportunity for public response to justify their inaction. The question should not be, "Why?" but rather, "Why not?"

2

The History of the Invitation

It is rather difficult to write a precise chapter on something which, after the apostolic era, had a new beginning which is clothed in ambiguity. In the post-New Testament era, changes occurred in the church which, both theologically and practically, made public invitations unnecessary. None of the words that we employ to describe the invitation—appeal, commitment, pledge, altar call, or invitation—is found in records of the New Testament nor are they found in the history of the church until the First Great Awakening in the thirteen colonies in the 1730s and 1740s. Though the exact words are not used, there is, nevertheless, solid evidence that the history of the church is punctuated with calls to public repentance, just as we have observed in the Bible.

Late Antiquity and Middle Ages

After the first two centuries of church history, the doctrine of salvation and the meaning of the word "faith" gradually underwent some very drastic changes. The church became the virtual depository of salvation. Faith became a matter of trusting one's soul to the church, which administered the sacraments through a priest. Salvation became sacramental, and with the union of church and state, the necessity of a public confession of faith was no longer needed.

To add further to the removal of the necessity of public decision, by the mid-200s the church began to baptize infants in some areas. These changes in doctrine completed the precluding of the necessity of extending a public invitation. With the wedding of church and state, basically all citizens of large geographic areas were baptized as infants and were considered Christians.[16]

In many instances when a king or tribal chief was converted to the faith, the entire tribe would simultaneously become Christian. A classic example is that of Clovis, King of the Franks. When he was converted to the faith, he had priests with palm leaves in their hands dipping them in water and sprinkling the water on his troops as they passed by. In this manner, the Franks became Christianized.[17] Conversion became a mass exercise. Ultimately, infant baptism became prevalent in the church and conversion was assumed by the church without any later experience required.

The only record of any kind of invitation being given in the Roman Catholic Church occurred in the twelfth century. An evangelical preacher in the church, Bernard of Clairvaux, in his call for genuine repentance would ask for a show of hands on the part of those who desired to be restored to God or His church.[18] It is possible that medieval evangelical groups which sprang up outside the Roman Catholic church—such as the Petrobrusians, the Waldensians, and the Bohemian brethren—did extend public invitations, but I know of no historical record to verify it.

Reformation

The doctrine of justification by faith was rediscovered by large segments of people through the Protestant Reformation. The major reformers, however, maintained a state-church relationship and continued to practice infant baptism. No public confession of faith was necessary.

With the Reformation came new drastic changes on the part of certain radical reformers who insisted that only true believers in Jesus were to be baptized. They repudiated the baptism of infants, contending that the New Testament taught that baptism was intended only for those who had trusted in Jesus. Historians have tagged these people with the name "Anabaptists." Albert Henry Newman calls attention to an Anabaptist meeting in the home of Ruedi Thomann:

> After much conversation and reading, Hans Bruggback stood up weeping, crying out that he was a great sinner and asking that they

pray God for him. Then Blaurock asked him whether he desired the grace of God. He said he did. Then Manz rose and said "Who will forbid that I should baptize him?" Blaurock answered, "No one." Then Manz took a dipper with water and baptized him in the name of the Father, Son and Holy Spirit.[19]

Thompson says that this scene is an illustration of Anabaptists extending a personal invitation after the gospel was preached. Regardless as to whether or not this picture is an incident of public invitation, any time a group of Christians demands that a baptized person must first be a believer, it is incumbent on that group to extend some type of invitation for public expression of interest. Otherwise, the group would not know whom to baptize.[20]

The Anabaptist preacher Balthassar Hubmaier baptized over five thousand people in one year in Nikolsberg, Moravia.[21] We may never know the exact nature of the kind of invitation Hubmaier offered, but some kind of opportunity for expression of interest is essential, whether one or several hundred are being baptized.

The same question that was raised about the experience at Pentecost must now be raised again: "How did those who were conducting the service and doing the baptizing know who to baptize out of the crowds who heard them?" Some call for public declaration was essential.

Post–Reformation

After the Reformation, pockets of preachers began to call people publicly to commit to Christ. Perhaps the practice of Anabaptists served as an example for these unnamed preachers. One whose name we do know is Claude Brousson. He was one of a number of French preachers forced out of France when Protestantism was made illegal in 1685. He returned to France three times to reestablish churches that had been decimated by persecution. He died as a martyr in 1698. In restoring apostates who had converted to Catholicism, he gave a public invitation for restoration:

> When the sermon was over, the preacher asked whether there was any among his hearers wishing to be reconciled to God and His church, and to re-enter the communion of saints . . . . Then, any who were so minded came forward and knelt before the preacher, who began to remonstrate with them and showed them how enormous was the sin they had committed in forsaking Christ. That being done, they were asked to say whether they did repent, and would henceforth live and die in the Reformed faith. In spite of the allurements and threats of the world; whether they heartily renounced the errors of the church of Rome, the Mass and all thereto appertaining . . . (This was done in much detail.) They had to answer Yes to all these questions, each individually. After this, they had to promise not to attend mass any more, and to take great care not to pollute themselves with Babylon, either by marriage or in other ways; not to allow their children to be trained in it, but, on the contrary, to instruct them in the principles of our religion. Each having duly promised, the ministers then proclaimed the remission of their sins, saying, "In the name and authority of Jesus Christ, and as a faithful minister of His Word, I declare to you the remission of all your sins, and there is now no condemnation for you since you are in Jesus Christ." Then followed a prayer on their behalf . . . . Forty-two of us were admitted in this manner, the rest of the flock having been received back at previous gatherings. The number of the communicants was about two hundred and fifty, men and women.[22]

Preachers of the First Great Awakening

The real roots of the public invitation as we know it today must be traced back to the First Great Awakening in this country in the eighteenth century. This awakening first laid the theological foundation for the emergence of the public invitation. As has been the case in other ecclesiastical issues, a change in theology led to a change in practice.

There is no record of any preacher ever calling people forward for decision after one of their messages during the awakening. However, in the early stages, there were at least two instances where response on the part of a congregation was so overwhelming and spontaneous that certain ones in the congregation came forward and became public seekers or inquirers. For instance, when Edwards preached his famous sermon, "Sinners in the Hands of an Angry God," at Enfield, Connecticut, July 8, 1741, a detailed account of what transpired, given by Stephen Williams, indicates that there was spontaneously a good amount of public expression of deep interest or immediate regeneration, and people were being dealt with in various parts of the building.[23] However, Edwards never made an appeal for public professions of faith, though he made appeals in his sermons for personal decisions.

A similar public expression occurred when Eleazer Wheelock, the founder of Dartmouth College, preached in Connecticut in October, 1741. Though it was not planned, it represents the clearest and perhaps the earliest instance of the preacher inviting people who are under deep conviction to come forward. The record comes from Thomas Prince, the nearest person to an on-the-spot historian of the First Great Awakening:

> In the afternoon, Wheelock preached a "close, searching experimental, awful and awakening" sermon . . . "he was delivering his discourse very pleasantly and moderately," the depth and strength of feeling increased, till "some began to cry out, both above and below, in awful distress and anguish of soul," upon which he raised his voice, that he might be heard above their outcries; but the distress and outcry spreading and increasing, his voice was at length so drowned out that he could not be heard. Wherefore, not being able to finish his sermon, with great apparent serenity and calmness of soul, "he called to the distressed, and desired them to gather themselves together in the body below. This he did, that he might the more conveniently . . . exhort them."[24]

Kendall makes a great deal out of this experience. He says,

> But what interests me also is this: the modern practice of calling people to the front (or whatever "the body of seats below" means) was apparently born in authentic revival . . . . This to me is weighty.

The very practice of the minister calling people to the front—by whatever name—was born in true revival. It was not born in a time of dryness. It was not born at a time when people were trying to manipulate people. The practice started in undoubted revival . . . . The modern practice of calling people forward began in real revival. You could say it had a spontaneous beginning.[25]

Though the invitations extended in the First Great Awakening were more spontaneous than planned, this awakening did lay the foundation for the type of invitation that evolved in the century to come. The number of sudden or instantaneous conversions virtually did away with the kind of Puritan morphology of conversion which had been a part of the strict Calvinistic theology of New England.

The awakening actually led great theologians and preachers like Jonathan Edwards to something of a new theology of conversion. This new theology in turn filtered into the thinking of Joseph Bellamy and Samuel Hopkins and in time led to the "new divinity" of Yale College and to a new concept of freedom of the will and original sin.[26] Incidentally, this new conception in turn led to an evolutionary theology of conversion which contributed to the thinking of the man who later did more to institutionalize public invitations than perhaps anybody in the history of the faith in the United States: Charles G. Finney.

Around the time of the First Great Awakening, it is believed that a group of Baptists who had settled in North Carolina were the initiators of the public invitation. They did it not in a spontaneous but in an intentional manner. We know this group as the Separate Baptists. This group was led by great preachers, who though generally not formally educated, were unusually gifted and endowed by the Spirit of God. The precise date is not known, but somewhere between 1755 and 1771—and it was likely more toward the earlier date—these men began to extend invitations at the end of their sermons. This practice appears to have characterized sizable elements of Baptist practice from that period on.

The prime mover of this group, Shubal Stearns, likely initiated this movement. Robert Devon, historian of North Carolina, describes the kind of invitation they extended at first:

At the close of the sermon, the minister would come down from the pulpit and while singing a suitable hymn would go around the brethren shaking hands. The hymn being sung, he would then, extend an invitation to such person anxiously inquiring the way of salvation, to come forward and kneel near the stand, or if they preferred to do so, they could kneel at their seats, proffering to unite with them in prayer for their conversion. After prayer, singing and exhortation, prolonged according to circumstances, the congregation would be dismissed to meet again at night . . . either for preaching or in the capacity of a prayer meeting.[27]

In 1785, in Tennessee, the great Baptist evangelist John Taylor felt led to call inquirers to the front of the church. He says about the experience: "When I stopped speaking, two men and their wives rose up and with trembling, came forward, and asked me to pray for them . . . . The thing being so new to people, it spread heavenly blaze through the assembly."[28] This account indicates that the practice of extending invitations in North Carolina had not yet become a widespread practice in the neighboring state of Tennessee.

The Methodists

With the conversion of John and Charles Wesley in 1738, new waves of spiritual life began to sweep across England and ultimately all of the British Isles. Although originally he opposed the idea, John Wesley began preaching to large crowds outdoors. Some contend that Wesley offered public invitations, but the evidence that public invitations were ever a part of the Wesleyan movement in England is extremely scanty.

A contemporary student of Wesley and author of an excellent Wesley biography, A. Skevington Wood, contends that Wesley always extended an invitation, but he never prescribed any kind of public demonstration to accompany it. A typical entry in his journal would be something like this:

While I was earnestly inviting all sinners to enter into the holiest by the new and living way, many of those that heard began to call upon God with strong cries and tears.[29]

But Wood says that there is no record of Wesley's prescribing any particular external form that an inner response should take. He did not invite people to come forward who wanted to receive Christ.[30]

Methodism in the United States took a different turn. In the nineteenth century, it became fairly standard procedure in Methodist churches to invite awakened sinners to the front, which came to be known as "the mourners' bench." Robert Coleman says this kind of "altar call" began first in the following way:

> The preacher then requested all that were under conviction to come together. Several men and women came, and fell upon their knees; and the preachers, for some time, kept singing, and exhorting the mourners to expect a blessing from the Lord, til the cries of the mourners became truly awful. Then prayer was made in behalf of for the mourners, and two or three found peace. My soul did magnify the Lord, and rejoice in God my Saviour.[31]

The gathering of convicted persons in a designated place where a minister might exhort while others sang represents a significant development in the emergence of the public invitation. According to Coleman, "It can be said that this marks the actual beginning of the contemporary 'altar call' procedure."[32]

By the time of the Great Awakening of 1800 and the establishment of camp meetings, the mourners' bench and the call to come forward were all regarded as standard procedure. Methodists in the nineteenth century never got away from these procedures and they became the fastest growing denomination in the United States. Though Methodists adopted the public invitation wholeheartedly after the Revival of 1800, it took another dramatic event in time to make the invitation a standard procedure in virtually every evangelical denomination. That event was the advent of Charles G. Finney as the most prominent evangelist in the first half of the nineteenth century.

Charles G. Finney

If any man in the history of evangelical American Christianity deserves to be called a spiritual watershed, it is Charles G. Finney. This holds true in both theology and practice. Methodists in frontier states with altar calls and a few Baptists fairly isolated in southern states giving public invitations did not carry enough weight to make a major impact on religious practices in this nation. This major change would require not merely strong personalities or even brilliant minds and unusual spiritual gifts, for both Methodists and Baptists had preachers who met these qualifications. It would require a ministry which penetrated significant parts of urban life in our country. When Finney's ministry moved out of rural areas of New York into what were then major cities—happening when new and strong winds of change were blowing in the United States—the ingredients were in place for major theological and practical changes in church ministry.[33]

After 1825, newspapers in the East began to carry news about Finney and the remarkable revivals he was experiencing. Finney's meteoric rise to fame was nothing short of spectacular. Theologically, the vast difference between Finney and prevalent Calvinistic thought is seen in Finney's doctrine of conversion as set forth in his memoirs:

> Instead of telling sinners to use the means of grace and pray for a new heart, we called on them to make themselves a new heart and spirit, we pressed the duty of instant surrender to God; we told them the spirit was striving with them to induce them now to give their hearts now to believe and to enter at once upon a life of devotion to Christ, of faith, of love, and Christian obedience. We taught them while they were praying for the Holy Spirit, they were constantly resisting him; and that if they would at once yield to their convictions and duty, they would be Christians.[34]

It was only a step from this belief system to incorporating immediate public confession of faith as part of the commitment this doctrine of conversion demanded.

After the great Rochester revival of 1831, Finney adopted anxious benches or anxious seats.[35] These anxious seats began as an experiment in which he invited people who were concerned about their salvation to come and sit on certain benches, usually at the front of an auditorium. This method became a standard for Finney's meetings.

Finney's "new measures," particularly the call to immediate public declaration, were not accepted without serious opposition. Asahel Nettleton, the first full-time American evangelist and a devout Calvinist, said about Finney and his followers, "They are driving us back into barbarism under the delusion of a new era."[36] He was joined in his opposition by Lyman Beecher, New England's most prominent pastor. But in time, Beecher joined the ranks of Finney's followers, and Nettleton's ministry had begun to seriously wane.[37]

By 1840, Finney and his "new measures" had virtually carried the field, and, primarily because of Finney's influence, a major evangelist could not be found in the United States after this period of time who did not in one way or another follow the "new measures" of Finney. All of them might not have gone as far toward Armenianism as Finney, but there were none of any significance who did not begin to employ public invitations of one type or another in their meetings. To my knowledge, no evangelist in any denomination of any stature since Finney has failed to give a public invitation of one kind or another. Thompson says about public invitations: "During this period, all the major denominations contributed to the ranks of the new profession. As the men carried their measures and their methods into the churches, the methods were adopted also by the pastors."[38]

3

The Rationale for Public Invitations

The biblical basis for pubic invitations is so strong that those who extend them do not need to defend the practice. Rather, they should be asking those who do not employ public invitations why they do not. What is found in the Bible is adequate rationale for extending an invitation to people to make an open declaration of spiritual commitment. There are, however, even more reasons for inviting people to make an open commitment. Exploring these reasons brings us to what Jesus said about public confession of commitment to Himself and also to the nature of the gospel and of human psychology.

Jesus' Emphasis on Public Confession

There can be no question about God's desire that His people always be willing to demonstrate that they are not ashamed of Him. When Jesus walked among us, He stated very plainly, "Therefore everyone who confesses Me before men, I will also confess him before My Father who is in heaven. But whoever denies Me before men, I will also deny him before My Father who is in heaven" (Matt. 10:32, 33 NASB).

The negative aspect of this challenge is repeated in an altogether different context in the book of Mark. There Jesus says, "For whoever is ashamed of Me and My words in this adulterous and sinful generation, the Son of Man will also be ashamed when He comes in the glory of His Father with the holy angels" (Mark 8:38).

Though these verses do not explicitly relate to public invitations, they do powerfully accentuate the fact that Jesus insists that His followers openly confess Him before other people. To Jesus, it appeared unthinkable that someone would claim allegiance to Him and be ashamed of it. In fact, the force of Jesus' words in these passages indicates that the person who is unwilling to confess Him before others really cannot claim a saving relationship with Him.

Kendall says if he had only one verse in the Bible to support the call for people to pledge themselves publicly to Christ, it would be those verses of "confessing me before men" in Matthew 10:32-33. And though these verses are not related in an explicit way to public invitation, a public invitation certainly offers a superb opportunity for one to stand up and be counted as a follower of Jesus.[39]

Some Hearers Are in "Harvest Mode"

Serious students of evangelism are aware that people who are not yet Christians fall into different stages regarding their willingness to respond to the gospel. Two of the first to formally describe these stages are Engel and Norton in their book *What's Gone Wrong with the Harvest?* They see lost people in one of six possible stages, each leading up to a commitment for Jesus. Some pastors and even some churches that have thought almost exclusively in terms of harvest are beginning to realize that there are people who are not yet in a harvest mode, and that sowing, watering, and cultivating are as much a part of evangelism as reaping.[40]

It is true that, periodically, a public invitation may result in the reaping of fruit that is not yet ripe. Conversely, the opposite effect is probably just as serious, if not more so. Some who are in a harvest mode may be discouraged if there is no opportunity for response. In every congregation of any size, there are some who are asking the question of the Philippian jailer, "What must I do to be saved?" (Acts 16:30 NASB). They are ready for harvest. To preach the gospel to these and not make an immediate offer of acceptance can be frustrating for them.

The opportunity for people to respond to the evangelistic invitation is simply a matter of allowing people who are in a harvest mode to do what they want to do. It may be that some preachers, through manipulation and a desire to appear "successful" on the basis of the number of people who come forward, have abused the public invitation at times. Still, it is a serious mistake to throw out the baby with the bath water. People who are ready to make a decision ought to be afforded the opportunity to do it.

Many Will Sincerely Respond

It often happens that someone will respond to a public invitation who had no intention of doing so when entering the service. While I was preaching in a church in the Dallas area, a young woman who was dressed in military uniform slipped into the service. I discovered later that she had simply been walking down the sidewalk in front of the church and, without having planned at all to do it, sensed very strongly that she ought to come in. She had virtually no church background, and when I extended the invitation, she was the first one who came forward to receive Christ.

Almost every preacher who has preached for any length of time has seen people with little or no Christian background brought to conversion by a gospel sermon coupled with a public invitation. Most of these people would not have been saved without an opportunity for open dedication. Kendall says:

> When the non-Christian knows that he has been asked to commit his life to Christ before he leaves the premises and do so publicly the pressure of the Holy Spirit will be on him from the start. It will not be human pressure. It is the pressure of the spirit . . . This brings the message home. He knows God is calling him to stand up and be counted. But, if there is no indication that he may have to put himself on the line, he will not be too worried about leaving the church as he came in.[41]

Invitations Season the Green Wood

In every congregation of any size, there are people who have never made a commitment to Jesus. They are at different stages in the process of moving toward serious consideration of their relationship with Jesus. When they observe someone making a public commitment to Jesus, that act can be a forceful factor in bringing them across the line for the Lord.

I have preached at times to people who didn't care at all about what I was saying. While I was preaching, they were most likely thinking, "When is he going to stop?" or "The game will begin in fifteen minutes. Why doesn't he let us out?"

In one such case, my message seemed to have fallen on hard ground; a particular listener thought he wasn't interested. When I extended an invitation, however, an adult man—seated on the pew immediately in front of my uninterested listener—slipped out from where he was standing and came forward to make an open confession of faith. Seeing this act made an impression that caused my listener in question to seriously consider his own spiritual condition.

My message did not get through to him at all, but when he saw one of his own peers responding, he was touched in a way that would lead him to give real thought about his relationship to God. He was "green wood"—unseasoned—but the impact of someone else's coming forward was being used to season him for later response. I heard Kendall say that before he began extending public invitations at Westminster Chapel in London, perhaps one person a year would seek him out in his study to inquire about how to become a Christian. But when he began extending invitations, one person a week would knock on his door wishing to know more about how to commit his or her life to Christ.

This change demands some serious inquiry. Why would the number of people, interested in becoming Christians and coming to his study, multiply? I believe the answer to that question is very simple. Many people do not realize that becoming a Christian requires a clear-cut decision to have Jesus as their Savior and Lord. Many people believe that they get into the Kingdom of God by the process of osmosis. But a public invitation can be used to clarify the fact that a decision to repent and believe is absolutely essential for receiving eternal life and becoming a genuine follower of Jesus.

The Nature of the Gospel

When one studies the message of the apostolic preachers, one conclusion that becomes obvious is that one distinction of New Testament preaching was that preaching and invitation were virtually inseparable. The very nature of the message the apostles preached compelled them to appeal for response. There are no instances of appeal without proclamation in apostolic preaching, but there are also no instances of proclamation without appeal. Michael Green, in *Evangelism in the Early Church*, observes that the apostles were not shy about asking people to decide for or against the God who had decided for them. They expected results.[42]

The gospel message is such that an invitation to respond is the logical outcome of its declaration. Though preaching is done primarily in the indicative mood, that is, stating the facts about Jesus, the imperative mood, calling for response, is also present. After his sermon at Pentecost, Peter called on his hearers to repent and be baptized (Acts 2:38). After his second recorded sermon, his imperative was "Repent therefore and be converted, that your sins may be blotted out" (Acts 3:19).

Jesus frequently coupled the indicative and the imperative. He would conclude a message with "unless you repent, you will all likewise perish" (Luke 13:3 NASB) or "Repent, and believe in the gospel" (Mark 1:15). His exhortation to several followers to "follow me" represents an imperative. Examining the nature of the gospel reveals that it represents an offer. God makes man a concrete offer of forgiveness of sin on the basis of the saving acts of His Son. Such an offer demands a decision. The good news of Jesus is of such a nature that it demands a verdict.

Because of this demand, the good news is incomplete without an appeal to respond. The very fact that it represents an offer implies the necessity of appeal. To refuse to urge someone to respond to the gospel would be similar to a salesman who, after eloquently describing his product and his benefits, leaves you without even inviting you to purchase it.

The Nature of People

By their very makeup, people need the opportunity to respond to the gospel. Someone has well said that "impression without expression can lead to depression." To preach for response and to fail to provide an opportunity for a commitment can frustrate those who hear the gospel and deepen them in their habit of procrastination.

By nature, human beings are spiritually lethargic. People need encouragement to respond to the offer of the gospel. Paul had a reputation as one who persuaded others. The Greek word *peithomen* for "persuade" is a strong word that is used to describe one aspect of his ministry: "Knowing, therefore, the terror of the Lord, we persuade men," Paul said in 2 Corinthians 5:11. People's innate tendency to put off can be checked through persuasion. Our inherent inclination to wait for a more convenient season will only be aggravated if there is no encouragement to decide. Favorable impressions may soon die if people leave without having acted upon deep impressions that they have felt.

The secular world has certainly recognized the necessity of appeal and persuasion to encourage people to act. All of us are acquainted with skillful and high-pressure methods of advertising. If we watched television for a twelve-hour period, we would be bombarded with scores of appeals to respond. The same can be said of radio, newspapers, magazines, billboards, and the internet. There has never been a more invitation-minded generation in history. There is nothing wrong with utilizing this invitation consciousness at every available opportunity for the sake of evangelism.

Some Will Decide for Christ

Through public invitations some people will decide for Christ who would not have otherwise done so. I sat one evening in the Municipal Stadium on the shores of Lake Erie in Cleveland, Ohio. Billy Graham had preached a twenty-minute sermon in a torrential rainstorm. When he extended the invitation, approximately fourteen hundred people came forward and stood in the rain around the infield area.

I asked myself, "How many of these people would have been saved had not Dr. Graham offered the invitation to come forward?" Undoubtedly, some would have made commitments where they sat, but I believe the opportunity for public acceptance led many to an initial decision who otherwise would not have made such a decision. Admittedly, premature response is a danger in asking for public commitments. This possibility must be balanced, however, against the possibility that failure to give opportunity for decision may keep many from making a decision for which they are ready. After the good news has been preached, many who hear are ready to openly commit themselves. The old adage "Strike while the iron is hot" is not inappropriate here. Impression without expression can lead to depression—and can result in a person's turning away from the gospel once and for all.

Invitations Are Psychologically Sound

Ralph Bell is quite correct in saying, "People need the opportunity for expression." He then quotes a psychiatrist who said, "What many people need today is an experience at an old-fashioned Methodist Mourners' Bench."[43] There is a psychological soundness in giving opportunity for public response. The eminent Christian psychologist William James said:

> Once the judgment is decided let a man commit himself, let him lay on himself the necessity of doing more, let him lay on himself the necessity of doing all. Let him take the public pledge if the case allows. Let him envelop his resolution with all the aids possible. Making a public commitment has a way of putting strength and fiber in a decision made privately in the heart. It is like driving down a spiritual stake that can amount to saying, "I'm burning bridges behind me, I'm cutting cables once and for all; I'm taking my stand for Christ and for right."[44]

In the July 1967 *Ecumenical Review,* Billy Graham made some interesting statements regarding the public invitation and the attitude of psychologists and psychiatrists toward it:

> I am often questioned why I ask people to "come forward" and make a public commitment! Certainly, this act is not necessary for "conversion." However, it has a sound psychological and biblical basis. I have had many psychologists and psychiatrists study my methods. They have criticized certain aspects of it, but one aspect that most of them commend is the invitation. Many of them have publicly written that this method is psychologically sound.[45]

Certainly, when such churches as the Roman Catholic Church or the Anglican Church invite people to come forward to receive the bread and wine, this too is an act of public commitment.

Graham adds in a footnote, "There is another psychological aspect, namely the basic human need to confess and pour out one's soul."[46] There is psychological soundness in coming forward. It is a strengthening factor to people to give them opportunities to declare openly what they are doing in their hearts.

4

How to Give an Effective Invitation

A theology student from England was sent by a professor to hear a noted preacher on the weekend. He came back with a kind of sophisticated disgust and said to his professor, "Why, that man didn't do anything but say, 'Come to Jesus.'"

"And did they come?" his professor gently inquired.

"Well, yes they did," the student grudgingly replied.

The professor then said, "I want you to go back and listen to that man preach again and again until you can say 'Come to Jesus' as he did and people respond."[47]

Give an Invitation with a Spiritually Prepared Mind

The importance of the invitation cannot be overstated. It is not merely an afterthought tacked on to the end of the sermon. The sermon should build toward those all-important moments when people will be asked to decide for Christ. Many of us extend invitations without ever giving serious consideration to the issues at stake. We would do well to remember that there is an awesome aspect to confronting an individual or a congregation with the offer of the Christian gospel.

Every soul to whom we present the claims of Christ is an eternity-bound person. Their decision about what we offer could and ultimately will affect their eternal destiny. The choice that will mean heaven or hell is made for many during the period of public invitation. These issues ought to be prayerfully pondered by the preacher before ever going into the pulpit.

But there is more involved than eternal destinies. Many people with whom we share Christ lead lonely lives. Christ can assuage that loneliness. Some who hear us have brought the fragments of their broken lives with them to the church, hoping to receive help. Jesus can put the pieces of broken lives together again. Peace, joy, purpose, removal of guilt: all are benefits which can be known by those who make an affirmative response to Christ. The initial step to knowing and experiencing these things can be made during the public invitation. These facts should saturate the mind of the one offering the invitation. This is giving the invitation with a spiritually prepared mind. Such preparation will be made in prayer. C. E. Autrey says:

> Let him pray until his greatest desire is to see the lost saved. Paul said, "Knowing therefore the terror of the Lord, we persuade men" (2 Cor. 5:11). Lost men are under the wrath of God (John 3:36). They are not aware of their condition. The evangelist knows this and must, by his firm, tender pleas, lead the sinner to realize his guilt before God. Mere perfunctory concern in the evangelist cannot be used of God to bring a sense of dire need in the sinner's heart.[48]

Extend the Invitation Confidently and Expectantly

I would address these questions to all who extend public invitations: "Do you really expect a response? Are you looking for something to happen?"

Every message should be preached and every invitation extended in the confidence that God wants things to happen. Here the simple element of faith comes into play. "According to your faith let it be to you," said Jesus to some who sought His blessing (Matt. 9:29). Many times, what happens when we invite people to Christ depends on what we expect to happen. As Jesus was unable to do mighty works at Nazareth because of their unbelief, likewise in our invitations He is unable to do mighty works if we do not believe.

On one occasion, a young student of Charles Spurgeon came to the great preacher complaining that he wasn't seeing conversions through his preaching. Spurgeon inquired, "Surely you don't expect conversions every time you preach, do you?"

The young man replied, "Well, I suppose not."

Spurgeon then said, "That's precisely why you are not having them."[49]

I am aware from experience there are many small congregations that do not hold a great deal of possibility for evangelistic response. In congregations which seem to change little in population, however, a pastor still has frequent opportunity for reaching someone through an evangelistic invitation. He also can vary the invitation to meet the congregation's needs.

Real expectation and confidence in God will seldom be disappointed. For this reason, in most congregations, it is not honoring the Lord to say Sunday after Sunday, "Isn't there one person here today who will respond to the claims of Christ and come?" Why not ask, "How many of you here today will receive Christ as your Savior?"

Rather than, "Won't you come," make it, "As you come, I will be here to greet you." Let the very words of your invitation express confidence and expectancy.

Give the Invitation Dependently

Real transformation of life in an invitation is not dependent on human contrivance but on the work of the Holy Spirit. He alone can convict of spiritual need. Only He can reveal Christ savingly. He is the only one who can perform the miracle which we call the new birth. Thus, the invitation should be given in dependence on Him. The fact that all of this is His work should be wonderful encouragement to us. He is anxious to do these things. Jesus promised, "He will testify of Me" (John 15:26).

I recall in my early ministry that I had great difficulty believing that the Holy Spirit was going to do these things through me. I'm sure that if some analyst psychoanalyzed me, he could have found factors in my background which made me question whether or not God would ever use me in the ministry of the gospel. I can recall at times, and I recall it with shame, that I would almost shake my fist toward heaven and say, "O God, we're going to have blessing in this service tonight in spite of you." At that time in my ministry, I had my pronouns all mixed up. My concept of Christian ministry was this: God is here for me to use in my ministry. Basically, it was selfish. Since that time, God has taught me to get my pronouns correctly rearranged. Now I realize that I am here for Him to use in His ministry. And He is very anxious to do this. He yearns to speak to people's hearts through us. He only wants us to trust Him to do it. Jesus said in John 7:38-39, "'He who believes in Me . . . "from his innermost being will flow rivers of living water."' But this He spoke of the Spirit" (NASB). For this reason, we should believe that the Holy Spirit is going to do His work and thus give the invitation in dependence on Him. We are channels through whom He works. Yielded to Him, we give Him opportunity to move in the lives of those to whom we preach.

Give the Invitation Clearly

I have marveled at how some preachers falsely assume that those who hear them actually understand what they are being asked to do in an invitation. More than once I have sat in services and heard the preacher say nothing more than, "How many of you will come?" People who have not been in church before are sure to be asking, "Come, but where?" or "Come, but why?"

In contrast, I have marveled at times at the clarity with which Billy Graham extended the invitation. He told people exactly what he wanted them to do and precisely how he wanted them to express that they were doing it. He was very explicit in giving his invitation and in specifying the manner in which he wanted people to express the fact that they were inviting Christ into their lives.

In our week-by-week invitation, God would have us be clear in telling people what we want them to do. When we invite people to receive Christ as their Savior and Lord, we should encourage them to make a specific public commitment of the fact that they are receiving Him. Something like this should be said: "This Sunday morning, if you are willing to turn from your sins and turn to Jesus Christ as Savior, I invite you to come out from where you're standing and come forward. I will be here to meet you at the front." We would add to this invitation the fact that some might want to join our church. We should be clear in inviting them to do so. The invitation can be expanded to include others who will sense the need of making a new commitment of their lives to Christ.

We should be specific in inviting them to make that commitment open and public. We should spell out precisely what we want people to do. A lack of specificity here can cheapen an evangelistic appeal. I heard of one lady who came forward. When she was asked by the preacher why she came, she said, "I don't know exactly, but I'm sure I can meet one of the appeals you mentioned in your invitation." In a sense, this vagueness subtracts from the luster of the gospel and can open the door of response so wide that almost anyone would have to come forward to maintain a sense of integrity.

Give the Invitation Honestly

Perhaps you have been in invitations where the pastor or evangelist has said, "We're going to have one more stanza," and before you know it one has become three or four or five. Most people in our congregations are still able to count. If you say, "We're going to sing two more stanzas and unless somebody comes we'll conclude the invitation," conclude the invitation if nobody comes after two stanzas.

If ever you have the impression that the invitation should be continued after making such a statement, express your feeling to the congregation. Ask them to forgive you as you retract the statement you made previously, but that you have confidence that they will understand. You sense the invitation should be extended just a bit longer. Be honest in giving your invitation.

Give the Invitation Courteously

It is difficult for me to envision the minister of the gospel being anything but courteous. Give the invitation with the love, patience, and gentleness of Christ. Don't scold, criticize, berate, chastise, or bully an audience. In my opinion, you will fail for certain in your invitation if you attempt any of these. If there is a time when tact and courtesy are the need of the hour, it's during the time of the invitation. A true minister of the gospel should remain sensitive to the feelings of people to whom he has been preaching. Be wary of unnecessarily embarrassing the people in a congregation.

I know one preacher who, in an invitation, asked all Christians to turn around and face the back of the auditorium. That left only those who were not Christians facing the front. This could be a fairly rude shock to some unsuspecting non-Christian who had come to hear the preacher that day. Maybe someone in that service would be so offended as to never come back.

Some preachers employ an invitation in which all who want prayer are to raise their hands. Then they make the mistake of putting extreme pressure on those who simply raised their hands for prayer. A hand raised for prayer is no excuse for bullying a person down the aisle.

Give the Invitation Thoroughly

Another aspect of giving an invitation is to take adequate time. John Bisagno, former pastor of First Baptist Church, Houston, suggested in a class lecture at Southwestern Seminary, "I have found that ninety percent of the converts come forward after the third verse of the invitation." Do not be discouraged if there is no immediate response as you make an appeal for Christ. Sometimes it takes more time for the Holy Spirit to do His work. I have observed a tendency in the early days of ministry to give invitations that are too lengthy. As we grow older, there is a tendency to be too brief. Reliance on the Holy Spirit regarding the length of the invitation is vital. Each one of us has had someone come and say after responding in the invitation, "I'm glad you sang one more stanza, for it was on that last stanza that I came to Christ." We must trust the Holy Spirit for leadership as to how long the invitation should be held.

Bisagno tells of an experience in his church when nine verses were sung without a single person coming forward. Most would have pronounced the benediction before nine verses without response. He went on to say when the invitation was completed, twenty-five minutes later, twenty-seven people had been converted, including nine adult men.

The change in the invitation song might be of some advantage here. If you believe the invitation should be extended, exhortation between stanzas of the invitation song could be profitable. It is important that we be in tune with the Holy Spirit in giving our invitations.

Give the Invitation Authoritatively

There is no reason to apologize for extending an invitation. We're inviting people to accept a quality of life they could never find anywhere else. The most sensible thing one could ever do would be to respond to our offer to receive Christ.

I have known some preachers who seem to bend over backwards to keep people from thinking they might be trying to persuade them to receive Christ as their Savior. Their attitude seems to imply something poisonous about conversion. It is almost as if they say, "We are sorry, dear friends, but we always offer an invitation for you to respond to the Christian gospel." Or, "We regret to inform you that at this time in our service we are going to sing a hymn, and you will have an opportunity to commit your life to Jesus Christ as your Savior and Lord." Such apologetic nonsense is a disgrace to the gospel we proclaim. What kind of Jesus are they trying to get people to respond to? There is no room for apology in extending an invitation for eternal life, and life abundant, in knowing Jesus.

Give the invitation authoritatively. I have marveled at times as I observed Billy Graham extending an invitation. You got the impression that he was almost ordering people to repent and believe. But why shouldn't he and why shouldn't we? We have the authority of heaven behind us when we call people to repentance. "[God] commands all men everywhere to repent" (Acts 17:30), and if we are preaching His Word in His name, so must we. A note of authority is one of the keys to a successful ministry; a lack of it one of the worst failures in giving an invitation.

Set your invitation on fire and people will come and watch the fire burn. As we invite them to break with the old life—a life which to many is a life of degradation, emptiness, and bondage—we call them to a life of freedom, forgiveness, and newness in Christ. With authority and without apology it should be done.

Give the Invitation Urgently

If we have any concept at all of the magnitude of the issues involved, urgency will characterize our invitation. The New Testament says, "Behold, now is the accepted time; behold, now is the day of salvation" (2 Cor. 6:2). Until one responds affirmatively to Jesus as Savior and Lord, one lives in rebellion against Him. Jesus is a King who is the rightful ruler of everyone's life. Until a person positively decides for Him as Lord and Savior, that person lives in revolt against the King. People should not be encouraged to leave the service without being brought face to face with their responsibility of responding to Christ. We should not invite them to go away and think over whether they are going to receive Him or not.

A classic story out of the life of Dwight L. Moody illustrates this urgency. One Sunday he gave his hearers the opportunity to leave the service and meditate on the question, "What will you do with Jesus?" At the close of the sermon, he said, "I wish you would take this text home with you and turn it over in your minds during the week, and at next Sabbath we will come to Calvary and the cross, and we will decide what to do with Jesus of Nazareth." Then he turned to Ira Sankey and asked him to sing a closing hymn. Sankey sang:

> *Today the Savior calls,*
> *For refuge now draw nigh*
> *The storm of justice fails*
> *And death is nigh.*[50]

The next morning much of the city of Chicago lay in ashes, for it was that fateful Sunday night of October 8, 1871, that Mrs. O'Leary's cow kicked a lantern over and the great Chicago fire began.

To his dying day, Moody regretted that he had told the congregation to wait. He later testified:

I have never dared to give an audience a week to think of their salvation since. If they were lost, they might rise up in judgment against me. I've never seen that congregation since. I will never meet those people until I meet them in another world. But I want to tell of one lesson I learned that night which I have never forgotten; and that is, when I preach, to press Christ upon the people then and there, and try to bring them to a decision on the spot. I would rather have that right hand cut off than to give an audience a week now to decide what to do with Jesus.[51]

5

Planning the Invitation

The importance of the invitation cannot be overemphasized. It is not something merely tacked on to the end of the sermon as an afterthought. The sermon should build toward those all-important moments when people will be asked to decide for Christ.

A preacher can explain at the beginning of his sermon that he will be giving an invitation at the close and then move on a constantly ascending line to his time of appeal. The songs, the prayers, and the sermon should all prepare the way for the invitation. To this point C. E. Matthews pointedly speaks:

How many people realize these facts? It might be said that the majority in the congregation and many of our ministers have little or no concept of the seriousness or the inexpressible importance of the invitation. This fact is revealed in the thing witnessed again and again at the conclusion of the preaching service: a good sermon, but no appeal. The audience stands; the people in the congregation begin fixing garments to make ready to leave . . . . The preacher as usual, in a cool and collected manner announces the number of the closing hymn with the stock statement: "We shall sing the first and last stanzas of the hymn. Should there be those present who wish to unite with the church in the manner in which we receive members, you may come forward as we sing." Could there be a greater tragedy than such a closing of a religious service? It is not inferred that there is any intended wrong in such an invitation, but one is almost persuaded that the devil himself could say amen to such an effort.[52]

This situation will not be the case if the preacher carefully plans the invitation.

I have a friend who, as an evangelist, claims that he gives as much time planning his invitations as he does his sermons. Watching him during an invitation proves he is not exaggerating his point. Yet many preachers have never considered varying the invitation. There are real possibilities for variety in the invitation; however, variety requires planning. A preacher should contemplate several factors when planning the invitation.

First, the major emphasis of a message should be stressed in an invitation. If you have preached on stewardship, the major stress of the invitation should be commitment to tithing or some other aspect of stewardship. If you have brought a message on the home, the invitation should include opportunity for commitment of homes to Christ. Such invitations could include specific challenges such as family prayer, or a time of daily devotions employing the Bible or some devotional book.

Second, when one preaches to the same small congregation every Sunday, a planned variety in the invitation can prohibit unnecessary monotony in the invitation, particularly where there are a limited number of evangelistic prospects. Almost every congregation includes people who have never made that decision to trust Jesus as Savior and Lord. As such, it is difficult to imagine planning an invitation that does not include an evangelistic appeal.

Since every sermon is not necessarily evangelistic, planning is vital if every sermon is going to conclude with an appeal for salvation. Regardless of the nature of the sermon, ending it with an appeal is always possible. For instance, a sermon on giving of material possessions can be turned in the direction of an evangelistic invitation by quoting a Scripture verse: "For you know the grace of our Lord Jesus Christ, that though He was rich, yet for your sakes He became poor, that you through His poverty might become rich" (2 Cor. 8:9).

Sermons aimed at comfort and support can be easily turned into an evangelistic appeal by making a statement such as this: "The Christ of comfort and consolation wants to come into your life. He loves you and offers himself today to be your Savior and constant friend." Invitations following messages calling for social involvement can be moved toward evangelism by stating that the greatest motivating factor toward social progress is the presence of the indwelling Christ in one's life.

Third, planning is desirable in case of an unusual response in an invitation. If the preacher extends the invitation for a lengthy period, the worship leader should be ready to change the invitation song. This contingency should be planned beforehand. I strongly encourage you, if you preach the gospel, to plan your invitation.

One of the strongest invitations I ever witnessed required a great deal of planning. The preacher of the evening concluded his message with an illustration about Robert Ingersoll, the noted agnostic from the state of Illinois. He related how Ingersoll would speak in cities all across the Midwest. He would preach on subjects such as "Why I Am Sure There Is Not a God," "The Mistakes of Moses," "Why Only a Fool Would Believe in Hell." He would proceed to build up straw men and then to tear them down.

One night in a midwestern city after Ingersoll had supposedly exploded any possibility that there might be validity in the Christian faith, he offered a challenge to his audience. He said something like this: "I am aware that many Christians come to hear me speak. I would like to ask who in this audience after I have spoken would still claim to be a Christian. After hearing what I said tonight, is there anybody here who will testify, 'I still believe?'" Not a soul stirred.

Ingersoll put his hands on his hips and laughed uproariously. He offered the challenge the second time: "Isn't there even one Christian here who will stand tonight and say, 'I still believe after hearing the great Ingersoll?'" Nobody responded. Again, Ingersoll laughed. He offered the challenge the third time. This time from one of the back rows of the theater, two teenage girls stood and began to move out the row and slowly down the aisle singing, "Stand up, stand up for Jesus, ye soldiers of the cross, / Lift high his royal banner, it must not suffer loss." As they walked, others slipped out from their rows and followed them until ultimately almost the entire audience was standing as one great throng in front of the stage singing in Ingersoll's face, "Stand Up, Stand Up for Jesus."

As the evangelist told the story, about halfway through, the instrumentalist began to play the song, "Stand Up, Stand Up for Jesus," a somewhat militant invitation hymn. By the time he had concluded the illustration, he went immediately into his invitation and invited all who were willing to stand up for Jesus by receiving Him as their Savior and Lord. I wasn't surprised when around seventy-five people responded. This represented a superb job of planning an invitation. Don't be afraid of innovation and creativity at this point.

Types of Invitation

Though most invitations involve an appeal to come forward, other types can be employed with great benefit. A preacher should have two or three types of invitation in mind and trust the Holy Spirit as to which he should use. I describe five possible invitations below, although the variations and combinations are numerous.

Invitation to Come Forward to Openly Confess Christ

In many evangelistic churches, the standard invitation is an invitation to come to the front of the worship center or sanctuary in acknowledgement of accepting Christ as Lord and Savior. This kind of invitation usually involves a word of counsel with the pastor and remaining at the front in order to be presented to the congregation. Most Southern Baptist churches have traditionally employed an invitation of this type. To all who employ this kind of invitation, a word of caution is in order. A clear distinction should be made between those who are coming merely as seekers and those who are making a definite commitment to Jesus. It is my opinion that a majority of those who come in response to an evangelistic invitation have not yet had a valid conversion experience when they make their journey from their seat to the front of the auditorium.

Some who come have been led to Christ previously, and some have really trusted Him during the message or invitation. But many come as seekers or as inquirers and should be counseled as such. Something in a sermon or invitation has convinced them that what the pastor is offering meets a need in their lives. In response to this awareness, they "walk the aisle." But the truth is that if they have not trusted Jesus as their Savior, the only thing that's really changed about that person is his location in the church. There's a desperate need for more than a handshake with the preacher and the filling out of a card. Failure to counsel with a person under these conditions is alarmingly presumptuous and represents an inexcusably careless dealing with souls. When there is any doubt as to whether or not a person has really trusted Jesus, the invitation to come forward should include an opportunity for individual counseling.

This danger was not as prevalent in the nineteenth century as it is now. There was a clear distinction made then between those who wanted to become Christians and those who already had become Christians and wanted to make an open confession of faith. The preacher invited those who wanted to become Christians to come forward for prayer and counsel. Then an invitation was extended for those who were sure they had trusted Jesus to come and openly confess their faith before the church. The danger today is that preachers are not creating a clear enough distinction between the two.

Invitation to a Counseling Room

I was walking out of a large church recently when I saw a large sign "Inquiry Room" on a door adjacent to the auditorium. Having grown up in an era of haphazard, hit or miss, slipshod counseling of people who came forward in an invitation, I was glad to see the sign, and realized it is reflective of the fact that churches, in general, are taking more seriously the matter of dealing with inquirers.

There are several ways an inquiry or counseling room could be used; I will mention two possibilities. First, the pastor could call attention to the room at the end of his message and invite people who are interested in knowing more about the Christian faith to stop by the room after the services are dismissed and they are leaving the auditorium. Needless to say, congenial well-trained counselors would be in the room to greet them.

A second way the room could be used would be that of taking people who come forward to the inquiry or counseling room immediately after they come forward. The pastor, after greeting someone who has come, would give them to an appropriate counselor who would take them to the room and talk with them in depth about the decision they are making. The use of counseling rooms necessitates a church having trained counselors who relieve the pastor of the responsibility of dealing with every one who comes. If several people respond in an invitation, traffic jams can occur in the "altar area," and this can at times be a hindrance to others coming in the invitation. Overall, an inquiry or counseling room probably provides the most intensive kind of counseling of any method of invitation. Life's biggest decision deserves this kind of thoroughness.

Because I was a victim of inadequate counseling, I am perhaps a bit sensitive at this point. At the age of nine I came forward wanting to become a Christian. Had somebody counseled with me, shown me my need of salvation and how to accept it, I probably would have been saved at that time. However, the only instruction I received was, "sit down and fill out this card." Later I was told to come for the baptismal service at such and such a time. Needless to say, such instructions did not point me to Christ and even at that time I sensed that not everything had happened to me that should have happened.

Over the years, the conviction deepened that I was not a true Christian. Though I had the outward "credentials," I had never had a saving experience with Christ. Almost ten years later, aware of my need of something I didn't have, I came forward again in a Baptist church to "be saved." This time I was greeted with "God bless you, we're glad you came," but again nobody took the trouble to show me how to trust Jesus.

A few months later, feeling a bit desperate, I went forward a third time with a very deep need to be right with God. This time I was told, "We will pray for you." For a third time in my life, I had come forward in an invitation in a Baptist church for the purpose of "being saved." Each time I left the services as lost as I was when I came in—lost, because nobody took the time to counsel with me and explain to me how to become a Christian. Shortly after this, standing on the front porch of my house, I understood clearly that I could be saved simply by trusting Jesus as my Savior, and I trusted Him then and there.

My own experience has convinced me that many other people who come forward might not know what they're doing either. Because of limited time and opportunity for counsel during the invitation on the pastor's part, every church of any size should have some well-trained counselors to assist the pastor in talking to people who come forward. I also prefer allowing adequate time for counseling outside the auditorium. Pastors should not rush to present people to the church in the same service during which they came forward if it means inadequate counseling.

Invitation to Fill Out a Card

In a day of innovative worship styles, many churches have ceased to invite people to come forward and confess faith. Some of the fastest growing as well as some of the largest churches in the United States have opted for giving people an opportunity to express interest by filling out a card or signing a perforated section of the bulletin. Such options as "I would like to know more about becoming a Christian" or "Today I prayed to receive Christ as my Savior" can be seen on cards in the backs of chairs or pews along with similar statements on an order of worship.

Many churches which give invitations of this nature wait until the end of the invitation to receive the offering, giving those who signed a card the opportunity to indicate it by leaving the symbol of their decision, the card, in the offering plate. Churches which employ this kind of invitation, as a rule, are very thorough in following up with phone calls or visits to those who have left a signed card in the offering plate. This method insures adequate time for counseling and appeals to those who are not ready to show their interest publicly.

Invitation to Raise One's Hand

In years gone by, a popular kind of invitation was asking people to raise their hand. When employing this kind of invitation with tact and discretion, it can greatly benefit those desiring spiritual help. While the congregation bows in prayer, the preacher invites all who sense their need and want to invite Christ into their lives to raise their hand to indicate this decision.

Invitation to Pray at One's Seat

Many people who have heard an evangelistic sermon or even an evangelistic appeal would like the opportunity to receive Christ, but many times they don't know exactly how to pray. The pastor can invite all who want to become Christians to follow him as he leads them in a "sinner's prayer." After explaining that he will lead them in a prayer to repent of their sins and accept Christ, he should slowly lead them to pray softly or silently after him in a prayer of this nature:

Dear Lord Jesus, I thank you that you love me and that you died to take away my sins. I admit that I am a sinner and I need you as my Savior. Come into my heart right now and forgive my sins. I trust in you to be my Savior and I depend on you to take me to heaven when I die. I will follow you as my Lord as long as I live. Thank you for hearing my prayer. Amen.

A wise pastor will, as a rule, employ more than one of these methods in an invitation. One pastor made use of four of them every Sunday. First, he would invite people who were not Christians or were not absolutely sure, to follow him in a "sinner's prayer" as he led them clause by clause from the pulpit. He then would invite all who prayed with him to come openly and confess that they had prayed to receive Christ. After this part of the invitation had ended, he would call attention to the part of the bulletin on which people could check a small box or a line indicating they had prayed the prayer with him but perhaps did not understand about coming forward. His fourth appeal was an invitation to stop by the inquiry or counseling room where in a very non-threatening environment people could learn more about what it means to know Jesus personally. Pastors who serve churches with two hundred or more in attendance should follow this example.

Psychology and the Invitation

Invitations are extended to people. Every sensible appeal should be made to lost humanity to receive salvation from Christ. From every legitimate basis the appeal should be made. The invitation to receive Christ should appeal to every human faculty possible. Thus, the power of psychology ought to be wisely employed in extending an invitation.

Psychology is the study of human nature and behavior. It involves knowledge of bases on which the people make response. It is concerned partially with the why and how of human response. Use of psychology is never to be abused to the degree that hearers make nothing more than a superficial response which comes short of genuine commitment to Christ. Yet if a preacher can make it easier for a person to make a sincere decision for Christ, this should be done.

The Psychology of Example

Perhaps a young couple comes forward to openly confess Christ as their Savior. You can stop the singing long enough to say: "Isn't it a wonderful thing to see a young couple openly commit themselves to Christ as Savior and Lord? Surely there are other young couples here today who ought to do the same thing. How many would follow this couple in publicly giving their lives to Christ?"

Perhaps a child comes forward; call attention to him or her and say something: "Here's a little boy, only ten years of age, whose heart was touched by the Savior. He has come forward to receive Him. God's way of salvation is so simple that a child can understand." After calling attention to the fact that certain people have come forward, one can begin singing again and give more people the opportunity to come forward.

The Psychology of Suggestion

If you're acquainted with your congregation and are aware that there are people there who need to make commitments to Christ, employ the psychology of suggestion. Perhaps there is a husband and a father who is not a Christian. Stop the invitation hymn and say something like this: "Isn't it a thrilling thing for a head of a household, a husband, a father to openly commit his life to Christ? I wonder how many husbands and fathers have never made that decision and they're here in this service tonight. How many of you right now will take your stand with God's people? Put your trust in Christ and openly confess Him. Come, even while we're singing."

The psychology of suggestion can also be helpful in encouraging Christians to win others to Christ. I recall that in a service one evening a Christian mother came down the aisle with a daughter who was unsaved. It was a wonderful sight to see. I called attention to it. I said simply, "I wonder if there are not other mothers who ought to lead their daughters to Christ, even as this mother has done tonight." I did not know another mother was there who had an unsaved teenage daughter. The next day the mother spoke to the teenage daughter about receiving Christ. That night, when another invitation was given, she had the happy privilege of walking down the aisle with that daughter as she openly confessed Christ at that service. This is the psychology of suggestion.

The power of psychology should never be employed merely to manipulate people to make an open response. In a highly charged atmosphere, playing on the emotions of people can gain public response which does not really involve the will in a surrender to Christ. Such careless trafficking with lives is inexcusable and an abuse of psychology in an invitation.

There are many people who need the Savior. Some of them will be attending your services. God can use a skillfully given invitation to lead them to make life's most important decision. God bless you as you offer that invitation!

6

Exhortation and the Invitation

When Peter's sermon at Pentecost pierced the armor of his hearers and struck a responsive chord, the New Testament says, "And with many other words he testified and exhorted them, saying, 'Be saved from this perverse generation'" (Acts 2:40). Though this part of his sermon is not recorded, it obviously was longer than just a sentence or two since Peter employed "many other words." Whereas the earlier part of his message had been a declaration of facts about Jesus coupled with an imperative to repent, this portion of his message was composed of an urgent appeal to respond to what he had said.

The King James Version uses the words "witness and exhort" to describe what Peter was doing. It appears that he was giving his audience good sound reasons why they ought to turn to Jesus. This part of his message was calculated to produce an immediate response on the part of his listeners. It amounted to why they should repent and turn to Jesus now.

In extending invitations today, exhortation is still a very viable part of our verbal appeal. Exhortation is a plea for action on the basis of sound reason. A pastor may appeal to a number of incentives that motivate people. Any one of these appeals might bring action since the influences which motivate the will are not the same with all people. There are a number of bases for motivation to action, each of which is consistent with the dignity of the gospel we preach. Several are listed and discussed below.

The Appeal to Self-Preservation

It is interesting to note that Peter's appeal to his first-century congregation was an appeal to self-preservation. He urged them to "save themselves" from the judgment which was coming on that crooked generation. Some psychologists have contended that man's strongest instinct is the instinct of self-preservation. What could speak more eloquently to this drive than the message of everlasting life? It is the privilege of the preacher of the gospel to show people that the kind of life Christ offers them can be experienced now and will never know end.

Some today question the wisdom of appealing to the emotion of fear, either in sermon or invitation. Though this should not be our primary basis of appeal, it is nonsense not to acquaint people with the dangers of spiritual procrastination or indifference. Jesus frequently employed appeals which warned of the consequences of refusal to repent and believe. I seriously doubt that we will improve much on what Jesus did. The same can be said of the apostles and the messages recorded in the New Testament which they preached.

The Appeal to the Highest Quality of Life

Many incentives to which one might appeal in invitations will have already been touched in the sermon. Pungent repetition of these motivating factors during the invitation can go a long way toward helping people to decide for Christ.

One of the finest appeals is to discover the highest quality of life possible. Jesus came to give us a salvation not only for the sweet by-and-by but for the nasty here and now as well. He offers to needy people life abundant. Appeal to those in your congregation whose lives are gripped by enervating anxiety and fear to exchange these for the people and joy Jesus can give. Tell those with heavy burdens to come to the One who wants to help us bear our burdens. Quote Matthew 11:28 during the invitation: "Come to Me, all you who labor and are heavy laden, and I will give you rest."

Paul Tillich has said that the three basic anxieties confronting modern men are guilt, meaninglessness, and death.[53] Ask people to find the answer to such anxieties through Jesus. Ultimate fulfillment in life comes through Him. Until a person comes to Christ, that person is living on a lower plane than that for which he or she was intended. Appeal to your congregation to accept the finest quality of life possible.

The Appeal to Recognition and Acceptance

In a day of unprecedented technical advances where technology has replaced human labor by the millions, there is a severe loss of identity and recognition. Many college students may feel that they are just a number among thousands. This is a serious jolt to human personality created in the image of God.

The invitation is a good time to remind individuals that "God knows you and He loves you. He has the hairs on your head numbered. He sees the sparrow fall, and you are of much more value than any sparrow" (Matt. 10:29-31). What a thrilling privilege to share with people who feel like an unimportant nobody that to God they are an important somebody. He loves them to the degree that He sent his Son to die for them. He recognizes them as people of worth and accepts them in his Son. This is a worthy appeal in any invitation.

The Appeal to Those Yearning for Freedom

One of the loud cries on the part of people in today's world has been a cry for freedom. Tragically, much of the freedom which people demand—freedom to do whatever they want—only leads to a deeper bondage. Real freedom is not freedom *to* sin but freedom *from* sin and its consequences. This freedom comes only from Jesus: "Therefore if the Son makes you free, you shall be free indeed" (John 8:36). There is freedom from sin's guilt, penalty, and power in Him. He offers freedom from anxiety and fear. He looses us from the fetters of selfishness which put us in bondage. We should appeal to people's longing for real freedom.

The Appeal to Fulfillment

Many people who hear us preach sense a real lack of fulfillment in life. They have tried many things for satisfaction only to be left empty after exhausting them all. The French philosopher Pascal has suggested that a God-shaped vacuum exists in human beings.

Until God fills the vacuum, people will always feel this inner emptiness. Those to whom we preach and to whom we appeal during the invitation need to be told that fulfillment will come only as Christ comes into their lives. He alone can fill the "God-shaped blank" in every person. Only then will people know satisfaction in life.

The Appeal to Adventure in Life

A basic drive in most lives is the yearning for adventure. Many people have never understood that God designed the Christian life to be adventurous. He didn't plan the Christian life to be a dull and monotonous routine. God planned for life in Christ to be a thrilling adventure. You can faithfully promise your congregation that if they will truly follow Jesus Christ as Lord, life will be punctuated with excitement and thrill. As one reads the book of Acts, one is struck that for New Testament Christians there was never a dull moment.

A great loss suffered by sizable segments of the professing church is this loss of emphasis on adventure and thrill that Jesus offers. The problem is not that these possibilities don't exist for those who follow Jesus; the problem is that our people have lost the concept of what it is to really follow Him. Nevertheless, an appeal in the invitation to know adventure and excitement is still an appeal one can rightfully make.

The Appeal to Influence

There is hardly a person who does not exercise influence over someone else. When a person decides to become a Christian, he or she influences someone else in this direction. We should appeal to people to make the decision to receive Jesus on this basis. Parents should be encouraged to get right with God for the sake of their family. The appeal to an unsaved father to "become a strong Christian influence to that son or daughter" can arrest him in his indifference and turn him to a positive response.

Studies indicate that in homes where both parents are Christians, usually all children in that family will become Christians. When one parent is a Christian, about half the children will be active Christians and half not. Tell people plainly that they are responsible to God for the way they influence others. Urge people to set the best example possible for friends, business associates, neighbors, and most importantly, their own family.

The Appeal to Supreme Duty

Someone has said, "The biggest word in the English language is the word 'duty.'" It is our duty to do what is right before God and our fellowman. The Scripture teaches that it is a human being's supreme duty to be right with God: "God commands all men everywhere to repent" (Acts 17:30). This is duty clearly specified. Some conscientious people will have their conscience pricked when they realize that they have neglected life's supreme duty. This appeal can lead them to God.

The Appeal to Gratitude

Many people do not realize that in turning down Jesus, they are turning down God's greatest gift. Though the words may sound severe, the basest form of ingratitude of which people are capable is to turn down God's offer of salvation. People who would not dream of being discourteous, rude, or ungrateful toward other people become this way to God by refusing to accept His gift of love in Christ.

In employing an appeal to gratitude, inquire of your congregation: "Have you thanked Jesus for dying for your sins on the cross?" Periodically, such questions can be used to awaken people to gratitude which will result in their giving their lives to Jesus.

The Appeal to the Need for a Friend

Jesus said to his followers, "No longer do I call you servants . . . but I have called you friends" (John 15:15). The Bible says, "there is a friend who sticks closer than a brother" (Prov. 18:24). Multitudes of people desperately need a strong friend in life to help them as they pass through a crisis.

A man whose wife had left him and his two daughters heard the statement that Jesus wanted to be a friend in a situation like that. Previously, he had been rather careless in his life of sin, but the experience he was going through sobered him to realize his need for a friend of great strength. When he heard about Jesus as a friend, he responded to the invitation to receive Jesus, and he found a friend who has been a great source of strength ever since. What a splendid basis of appeal to needy people.

V. L. Stanfield suggests a list of contrasts that fairly well sum up the bases of our appeal to people to respond to Jesus as their Savior. The contrasts he lists are pictured in the chart below.[54]

Positive	Negative
Assurance	Fear
Fellowship	Loneliness
Purpose	Lack of Meaning
Peace	Inner Conflict
Strength	Weakness
Certainty	Uncertainty
Changeless	Changing
Forgiveness	Guilt
Heaven	Hell

Eternal Life	Eternal Separation
Life	Death
At Home	Away from Home
[Courage]	Cowardice
Fair Play	Unfair Play
Normal	Abnormal
Reasonable	Unreasonable

Though this list does not exhaust all possible motives and instincts to which we may appeal, the basic ones are there. Creative ingenuity will aid you to list others and will amplify ways of using the ones listed here.

7

Worship Songs and the Invitation

In the few books available about the invitation, little is written about music during the invitation. If rightly employed, songs can be a great asset in helping people to decide for Christ. Before reaching my teens, I heard the great evangelist Charlie Taylor preach. I don't remember anything about the sermon, but I was tremendously moved by the hymn of invitation. I still remember the words:

> *O don't go away without Jesus.*
> *Don't go away without him,*
> *You know he is willing to save you and*
> *cleanse from your heart every sin.*
> *O take of his infinite mercy*
> *O yield to the grace he imparts*
> *and don't go away without*
> *Jesus in your heart.*[55]

Though I didn't realize the significance of that part of the service, the lyrics of the hymn stayed with me for a long time and made me wish that Jesus was really in my heart.

As the history of the modern invitation is somewhat clouded in obscurity, so also is the history of the invitation hymn.[56] Likely, the first preacher who made use of a hymn specifically designed for an invitation to public profession was Charles G. Finney. In the great revival in Broadway Tabernacle in New York City, Finney began to employ a hymn especially designed for an invitation. The music was led by Thomas Hastings (who wrote "Rock of Ages"), and the hymn was sung as Finney invited people to come and sit in the "anxious benches." The words of Finney's standard invitation hymn were moving:

> Hearts of stone, relent, relent,
> Break, by Jesus' cross subdued;
> See his body, mangled—rent
> Covered with a gore of blood.
> Sinful soul, what has thou done!
> Murdered God's eternal Son.
> Yes, our sins have done the deed,
> Drove the nails that fixed him there,
> Crowned with thorns his sacred head,
> Pierced him with a soldier's spear;
> Made his soul a sacrifice,
> For a sinful world he dies
> Will you let him die in vain,
> Still to death pursue your Lord;
> Open tear his wounds again,
> Trample on his precious blood?
> No! with all my sins I'll part,
> Savior, take my broken heart.[57]

After Finney, most musicians who worked with a vocational evangelist appeared to have made use of invitation hymns.[58] During the time of Finney's ministry, Charlotte Elliot wrote the invitation hymn "Just as I Am," but it never came to prominence as an invitation hymn until the revival of 1858.[59]

Southern Baptist churches have for most of their history extended public invitations. Some idea of the influence of invitation hymns in Southern Baptist churches is seen in modern hymnals. There are over forty invitation hymns in the Baptist hymnal of 1975 and over fifty in the one published in 1991.[60]

WORSHIP SONGS AND THE INVITATION

Since moving from sermon to invitation represents a major transition in a service, this part of the service should never be taken lightly or casually planned. Many preachers find that making the transition from the sermon to the invitation to be a bit difficult. Because this is a crucial matter, the worship team should give special attention to it. The preacher and his team cannot afford to be careless at this point. The Holy Spirit overrules our clumsiness at times, and there are unusual results in response to an invitation in spite of our mistakes, but planning helps in making the transition.

Many preachers prefer to conclude their message with prayer. If this is done, it provides a good method of transition to the period of invitation. After praying, the preacher can explain the decisions he will call for in the invitation. Many pastors and evangelists prefer soft instrumental music during the prayer and continuing through the preacher's explanation of what will happen in the invitation. The instrumental music can lead into the invitation song which will be sung by the congregation, choir, or worship band.

A system of understood signals between the pastor and worship leader can be helpful at this point. When the preacher is ready for a choir or the congregation to begin singing, he can inconspicuously signal the worship leader, who will begin singing immediately. After a pastor and worship leader have been working together for a number of weeks, the worship leader will usually know precisely when to begin.

It is quite true that other preachers prefer to enter into the invitation without concluding their message with prayer. Regardless of the conclusion of the sermon, through adequate planning, it can always correlate to the importance of commitment to Christ. The worship band or accompanist will need to begin playing softly at the proper time while the pastor or evangelist is stating what he wants the congregation to do in response to his invitation. Avoid pompous instrumental introductions to the invitation song; they only distract from the invitation.

Regardless of one's choice of music, the worship leader should never lead the congregation by waving his or her arm. This can distract from the invitation as well. Avoid announcing the number in the hymn book if the church uses hymnals. Minimize fumbling over pages in the hymn book during this strategic time in the service since it can take away from the vital issues at hand. In many—perhaps most—churches today the words of an invitation song are shown on the screen. This can be very helpful. If no screen is available, the words to a particular invitation hymn or chorus could be printed in an order of service in the appropriate part of the bulletin. Personally, I prefer that the congregation have their heads raised looking at a screen rather than looking down at a book or a printed invitation. Regardless of the method, smoothness and flow is crucial. Those who have extended invitations over the years understand the vital importance of this subject.

I realize that hymnals in many churches have been replaced with power point presentations and projectors. Along with this shift has come a serious change in the type of music used in many invitations. Traditionally, hymns of invitation have been strong in the element of appeal. They encourage people to make a response. "Just as I Am," the best known invitation hymn in modern history, appeals to a congregation to come to Jesus. "Softly and Tenderly" encourages people to come home to God. "Have Thine Own Way" challenges people to give their lives completely to God.

Such appeals are not included in the invitation songs seen on screens in most auditoriums today. Regardless of the type of song, the words should include an exhortation for people to give their heart and life to Jesus.

My personal experience leads me to regard invitation hymns as a crucial part of the service and to believe the element of appeal should be part of the lyrics of the song, hymn, or chorus that is sung during the invitation. At the time when I became a Christian, I was almost twenty and had been in church all of my life. I still did not know how to be saved. I finally came to a place of deep desire to be saved, and I simply did not know how. After two sleepless nights, I stood on the front porch of my house around noon, struggling to find the way to God. I knew very few verses of Scripture, so it was not Scripture that came to my mind. The truth came to me through the words of the invitation hymn that had been sung the last

Sunday evening I had been in church:

> *Only trust Him, only trust Him,*
> *Only trust Him now;*
> *He will save you, He will save you,*
> *He will save you now.*[61]

For the first time, I understood that Jesus would save me if I only trusted Him to do it. Then and there I put my trust in Jesus as my Savior, and He radically changed my life from that day forward.

Epilogue
By Steve Fish

Inviting people to come into a personal relationship with Jesus was Roy Fish's passion. To my father, giving someone the opportunity to respond to the gospel wasn't a duty; it was his heart's deepest desire. Sharing the gospel wasn't something that he considered a profession; it was his passion. All over the world, people have shared the impact that my dad had on their life. He led thousands to the Lord and equipped countless others to live a lifestyle of sharing the gospel.

Several days before Dad passed away, he lay in a hospital bed after a week of being in and out of intensive care. That afternoon Dad and I had a wonderful conversation. His health had improved some, and it looked like he might come home the next day. I had no idea it would be my last extended conversation with him. What precious moments those were!

As we were conversing, a nurse came into the room and then left. At that moment Dad said to me, "Son, I've had a lot of nurses this week and everyone one of them knows the Lord except that one." During an incredibly intense week of life-and-death health challenges, most of the time wearing an oxygen mask, Dad still made the effort to converse with and assess the spiritual condition of every one of his nurses.

However, Dad did not simply do that because he was in the hospital. I watched him live his entire life that way. Whether in a hospital room or a gas station, a restaurant or a pulpit, he lovingly and confidently shared the message and gave an invitation.

One day Dad and I were fishing in a small boat on the pond behind his home. As we sat there, he began to share with me about the spiritual condition of all his neighbors. That day, it was clearer to me than ever before that he deeply loved his neighbors, was praying for them and looking for every opportunity to share Christ with them. Just a few weeks ago another person approached me . . . another one whose life was changed because Roy Fish unashamedly chose to give one more opportunity, one more invitation to come into a relationship with Christ.

On September 10, 2012, Dad went to heaven to be with the Jesus that he so loves. However, the legacy of the life of Roy Fish did not go with him to the grave. It lives today and is available to those who will receive Him. The seeds planted through his life were not in vain. They will grow and multiply and multiply.

The invitation still stands today. The invitation to live a life of lovingly and boldly inviting others to know Jesus still stands.

I'm forever grateful that on May 21, 1971, in the back room of our home, Roy Fish, my dad, extended an invitation to me.

Endnotes

[1] R.T. Kendall, *Stand Up and Be Counted* (London: Hopper and Stoughton, 1984), 37.

[2] W. Oscar Thompson, *The Public Invitation as a Method of Evangelism: Its Origin and Development* (PhD diss., Southwestern Baptist Theological Seminary, 1979).

[3] Roy J. Fish, *Giving a Good Invitation* (Nashville: Broadman Press, 1974).

[4] R. Alan Streett, *The Effective Invitation* (Grand Rapids, Michigan: K Regel Publications, 1984).

[5] O. S. Hawkins, *Drawing the Net* (Nashville: Broadman Press, 1993).

[6] Kendall, *Stand Up and Be Counted.*

[7] David Bennett, *The Altar Call: Its Origins and Present Usage* (University Press, 2000).

[8] Faris D. Whitesell, *Sixty-Five Ways to Give Evangelistic Invitations* (Grand Rapids: Zondervan, 1945), 12.

[9] Kendall, *Stand Up and Be Counted,* 44.

[10] Ibid.

[11] Whitesell, *Sixty-Five Ways,* 13.

[12] Thompson, *The Public Invitation,* 7.

[13] Frederick William Danker, ed., *A Greek English Lexicon of the New Testament and Other Christian Literature* (Chicago: University of Chicago Press, 2000), 764.

[14] C. E. Autrey, *Basic Evangelism* (Grand Rapids: Zondervan, 1959), 127-128.

[15] Whitesell, *Sixty-Five Ways,* 15.

[16] Philip Schaff, *History of the Christian Church*, 5th ed., vol. 2, *Ante-Nicene Christianity. A.D. 100-325* (New York: Charles Scribner's Sons, 1889), 166.

[17] William Stearns Davis, ed., *Readings in Ancient History: Illustrative Extracts from the Sources*, 2 vols., (Boston: Allyn and Bacon, 1912-1913), 331-337. In "Medieval Source Book," ed. Paul Halsall, last modified August 1998, http://www.fordham.edu/Halsall/source/496clovis.asp.

[18] L. M. Perry and J. R. Strubhar, *Evangelistic Preaching* (Chicago: Moody Press, 1979), 44.

[19] Albert Henry Newman, *A History of Anti-pedobaptism* (Philadelphia: American Baptist Publication Society, 1896), 107.

[20] Thompson, *The Public Invitation, 19.*

[21] Henry C. Vedder, *Balthasar Hübmaier, the Leader of the Anabaptists* (New York: G. P. Putnam's Sons, 1905), 152-153.

[22] Translated and quoted by Rubens Saillens, *The Soul of France* (London: Morgan and Scott, 1917), 85-87.

[23] Joseph Tracy, *The Great Awakening* (Boston: Charles Tappan, 1845), 216.

[24] Ibid., 167.

[25] Kendall, *Stand Up and Be Counted,* 47-48.

[26] Joseph A. Conforti, *Samuel Hopkins and the New Divinity movement: Calvinism, the Congregational Ministry, and Reform in New England Between the Great Awakenings* (Grand Rapids: Christian University Press, 1981).

[27] Robert I. Devon, *A History of the Grassy Creek Baptist Church* (Raleigh, N.C.: Edwards, Broughton, & Co., 1880), 59-60.

[28] Streett, *The Effective Invitation,* 94.

[29] John Wesley, *The Works of John Wesley*, vol. 1, (Philadelphia: D. & S. Neall and W. S. Stockton, 1826), 266.

[30] A. Skevington Wood, *The Burning Heart: John Wesley, Evangelist* (Grand Rapids:Wm. B. Eerdmans, 1967), 160-161.

ENDNOTES

[31] Robert E. Coleman, "The Origin of the Altar Call in American Methodism," *The Asbury Seminarian* (Winter 1958), 22.

[32] Ibid.

[33] "From the Editor: Father of Modern Revivalism," *Christian History*, no. 20 (1988), last modified October 1, 1998, http://www.christianitytoday.com/ch/1988/isue20/2002.html?start=2.

[34] Charles G. Finney, *Memoirs of Rev. Charles G. Finney* (New York: A. S. Barnes & Company, 1876), 189.

[35] G. Frederick Wright, *Charles Grandison Finney* (Boston: Houghton and Mifflin, 1893), 100-103.

[36] Robert Samuel Fletcher, *A History of Oberlin College: From Its Foundation Through the Civil War*, vol. 1, (1943: New York: Arno Press & The New York Times: New York, 1971), 16.

[37] Wright, *Charles Grandison Finney*, 74-75, 104-105.

[38] Thompson, *The Public Invitation*, 111.

[39] Kendall, *Stand Up and Be Counted*, 23.

[40] James F. Engel and H. Wilbert Norton, *What's Gone Wrong with the Harvest? A Communication Strategy for the church and World Evangelization* (Grand Rapids: Zondervan Publishing, 1975).

[41] Kendall, *Stand Up and Be Counted*, 23.

[42] Michael Green, *Evangelism in the Early Church*, rev. ed. (Grand Rapids: Wm. B. Eerdmans, 2003), 212.

[43] Ralph Bell, "Giving a Successful Invitation: Preaching for a Verdict," in *NACIE 94 Equipping for Evangelism: North American Conference for Itinerant Evangelists*, ed. Charles Ward (Minneapolis: World Wide Publications, 1996), 83.

[44] Quoted from Leighton Ford, *The Christian Persuader* (New York: Harper & Row, 1966), 124.

[45] Billy Graham, "Conversion – a Personal Revolution," *Ecumenical Review* 19, no. 3 (July 1967): 276.

[46] Ibid.

[47] Ford, *The Christian Persuader*, 139.

[48] C. E. Autrey, *Basic Evangelism* (Grand Rapids: Zondervan, 1959), 132.

[49] W. Y. Fullerton, *C.H. Spurgeon: A Biography* (London: William and Norgate, 1920), 232-233.

[50] "Today the Savior Calls, Ye Wanderers Come," by Samuel Francis Smith.

[51] From Clarence Macartney, *The Greatest Questions of the Bible and of Life* (Nashville: Abingdon-Cokesbury), 93.

[52] C. E. Matthews, *The Southern Baptist Program of Evangelism* (Nashville: Convention Press, 1956), 93.

[53] Paul Tillich, *The Courage To Be* (London: Collins, 1952).

[54] V. L. Stanfield, *Effective Evangelistic Preaching* (Grand Rapids: Baker Book House, 1965), 35.

[55] This song comes from a hymnbook edited by Laurie Taylor.

[56] Though singing occurred during the altar calls in the early nineteenth century camp meetings, these were not looked on as hymns of invitation.

[57] Richard Manzelman, *The Revival Heard Around the World* (New York: Auburn Theological Seminary, 1975), 30.

[58] This would include the teams of Moody and Sankey, Chapman and Alexander, Sunday and Rodeheaver, Mordecai Ham and W.J. Ramsay, and Billy Graham and Cliff Barrows.

[59] Roy J. Fish, *When Heaven Touched Earth; the Awakening of 1858 and Its Effects on Baptists* (Azle, TX: Need of the Times Publishers, 1996), 198.

[60] *Baptist Hymnal* (Nashville: Convention Press, 1975); *The Baptist Hymnal* (Nashville: Convention Press, 1991).

[61] "Only Trust Him," by John H. Stockton, 1873.

CPSIA information can be obtained
at www.ICGtesting.com
Printed in the USA
LVHW022139190820
663618LV00013B/1445